DEVOTIONS
for
SUNDAY
SCHOOL
TEACHERS
2

DEVOTIONS
for
SUNDAY
SCHOOL
TEACHERS 2

Stan Toler
John C. Baldwin
David W. Graves

BEACON HILL PRESS
OF KANSAS CITY

ISBN-13: 978-0-8341-2323-6
ISBN-10: 0-8341-2323-1

Printed in the
United States of America

Cover Design: Darlene Filley
Interior Design: Sharon Page

All Scripture quotations not otherwise designated are from the *Holy Bible, New International Version®* (NIV®). Copyright © 1973, 1978, 1984 by the International Bible Society. Used by permission of Zondervan Publishing House. All rights reserved.

Scripture quotations marked KJV are from the King James Version of the Bible.

Scripture quotation marked PHILLIPS is reprinted with the permission of the Macmillar Publishing Company from *The New Testament in Modern English* (PHILLIPS), Revised Student Edition, by J. B. Phillips, translator. Copyright 1958, 1960, 1972 by J. B. Phillips.

Library of Congress Cataloging-in-Publication Data

Toler, Stan.
    Devotions for Sunday school teachers 2 / Stan Toler, John C. Baldwin, David W. Graves.
        p. cm.
    ISBN-13: 978-0-8341-2323-6 (pbk.)
    ISBN-10: 0-8341-2323-1 (pbk.)
    1. Sunday school teachers—Prayers and devotions. I. Baldwin, John C. II. Graves, David W., 1953- III. Title.

    BV4596.S9T65 2007
    242'.69—dc22

                                                                2007017662

10 9 8 7 6 5 4 3 2 1

CONTENTS

ABOUT THE AUTHORS

John C. Baldwin has been a commercial banker for more than 35 years and is a regular lecturer/instructor at numerous national and state association-sponsored banking schools and seminars. He is an active church layman who serves on local and sistrict boards. For the past 15 years he has led the Cliffhangers Adult Sunday School Class at Highland Park Church of the Nazarene in Lakeland, Florida. He coauthored *Devotions for Sunday School Teachers* (Beacon Hill Press of Kansas City) and has written hundreds of adult-level Bible studies and series for Sunday School application. He and his wife, Glenda, live in Riverview, Florida.

For additional information or to contact John Baldwin:
John C. Baldwin
P. O. Box 3370
Tampa, FL 33601-3370
merfb@aol.com

David W. Graves serves as senior pastor at College Church of the Nazarene in Olathe, Kansas. He previously served as director of Sunday School Ministries for the Church of the Nazarene International Headquarters. He has pastored in Ohio, Tennessee, Oklahoma, and North Carolina. Dr. Graves graduated from Olivet Nazarene University, earned a master of divinity degree from Nazarene Theological Seminary, and received an honorary doctorate of divinity degree from Olivet Nazarene University. He and his wife, Sharon, currently reside in Overland Park, Kansas.

For additional information or to contact David Graves:
David W. Graves
2020 E. Sheridan
Olathe, KS 66062
davidgraves@collegechurch.com

Stan Toler is senior pastor of Trinity Church of the Nazarene in Oklahoma City, where a new 1,000-seat sanctuary was recently constructed. For several years he taught seminars for Dr. John Maxwell's INJOY Group—a leadership development institute. He also serves as the executive director of the Toler Leadership Center, located on the campus of Mid-America Christian University. Toler has written more than 60 books, including his best-sellers *God Has Never Failed Me, but He Sure Has Scared Me to Death a Few Times; The Buzzards Are Circling, but God's Not Finished with Me Yet; God's Never Late, He's Seldom Early, He's Always Right On Time;* his popular *Minute Motivators; The Secret Blend;* and his latest book, *Practical Guide to Pastoral Ministry.* Toler is the co-founder of BGW Forward in Faith and was recently elected to the position of senior associate for stewardship with the Lausanne Committee for World Evangelism.

For additional information on seminars,
scheduling speaking engagements, or to contact Stan Toler:
Stan Toler
P. O. Box 892170
Oklahoma City, OK 73189-2170
E-mail: stoler1107@aol.com
Web site: www.StanToler.com
www.BuildingGodsWay.com

ACKNOWLEDGMENTS

Special thanks to Deloris Leonard, Pat Diamond,
Jerry Brecheisen, Bonnie Perry, Barry Russell,
and the Beacon Hill Press team.

FOREWORD

The Master Teacher invites you to spend some precious moments with Him and His good Word today. As you seek fellowship with the One who is with you always, rejoice that He knows you and all about your circumstances.

The devotional thoughts and truths in this second volume of devotions for Sunday School teachers will speak to the profound issues of your life. They will energize and resource you as you discover His peace and strength for today. Beginning or ending your day with these truths and thoughts will be a refreshing breath for your soul.

As a Sunday School teacher, you touch folks from all walks of life who may have no uplifting thoughts to fill their hearts and minds. Many may struggle with secret anxieties and quiet despair as they search for solutions to life's challenges. In their isolation, loneliness, and unspoken restlessness, they need a teacher who has found a meaningful and satisfying relationship with God and others.

As the Lord uses this devotional book to refresh your spirit, I encourage you to intentionally pass on the inspiration to someone else. Could it be that the blessings you receive from this quiet time are not to stop with you?

The Lord may be preparing someone who needs your refreshing words of love, acceptance, and friendship today. Enjoy the blessings of these devotional insights and then share the joy with those you touch.

Thank you for your faithful service in the Kingdom.

Woodie J. Stevens, Director
Sunday School and Discipleship Ministries International
Church of the Nazarene

WE WAIT FOR THE BLESSED HOPE—THE GLORIOUS
APPEARING OF OUR GREAT GOD AND SAVIOR,
JESUS CHRIST, WHO GAVE HIMSELF FOR US TO
REDEEM US FROM ALL WICKEDNESS AND TO PURIFY
FOR HIMSELF A PEOPLE THAT ARE HIS VERY OWN,
EAGER TO DO WHAT IS GOOD.
—Titus 2:13-14

BECAUSE CHRIST DIED AND RESCUED US FROM SIN,
WE ARE FREE FROM SIN'S CONTROL. THE HOLY SPIRIT
GIVES US THE POWER AND STRENGTH TO LIVE
ACCORDING TO HIS WILL AND TO DO GOOD.
THEN WE WILL LOOK FORWARD TO CHRIST'S
WONDERFUL RETURN WITH
EAGER EXPECTATION AND HOPE.

LET THE WORD OF CHRIST DWELL IN YOU RICHLY
AS YOU TEACH AND ADMONISH ONE ANOTHER
WITH ALL WISDOM, AND AS YOU SING PSALMS,
HYMNS AND SPIRITUAL SONGS WITH GRATITUDE
IN YOUR HEARTS TO GOD.
—Col. 3:16

THE BIBLE WILL KEEP YOU FROM SIN,
OR SIN WILL KEEP YOU FROM THE BIBLE.
—D. L. Moody

LOVE FOR GOD'S WORD

I have hidden your word in my heart that I might not sin against you.
—Ps. 119:11

Psalm 119 has the distinction of being the longest chapter in the Bible. Its 176 verses are arranged in 22 sets of 8 verses each. Each section begins with a different letter of the Hebrew alphabet. Bible scholars have long marveled at this psalm's masterful literary construction. But the greatest marvel is that the entire psalm dwells on the psalmist's insatiable love for God's Word.

After reading this incredible psalm, we find it natural to do a bit of self-reflection. Do I love God's Word as much as the psalmist? Does it mean as much to me as to him? Has God's Word had a profound impact on my life? Compared to other activities, what percentage of my time do I spend in serious, focused dwelling on God's Word? Has my affection for and dedication to what God has told us in the Bible influenced those in my Sunday School class to a similar love?

There's an almost limitless number of things we can do each Sunday in our classes. Many of these activities are of some use and benefit in our roles as leaders and teachers. Most could be generously considered spiritual entertainment.

Nothing we might do each Sunday is more profitable or eternally important than carefully and systematically exposing our classes to God's Word. The answer to every perplexity and question in life can be found in the Bible.

God's Word is an inexhaustible mine of comfort, aid, instruction, hope, and guidance in all of life's limitless challenges. Take great care to ground every lesson on the solid rock of God's Holy Word. Cultivate in your class a love and hunger for God's Word. Read it, study it, and live it!

Prayer: *Father, cultivate in me a love and desire for your Word. Help me to be the catalyst for developing the psalmist's passion for the Bible in my class. In Jesus' name. Amen.*

ALTOGETHER, ENOCH LIVED 365 YEARS.
ENOCH WALKED WITH GOD; THEN HE WAS NO MORE,
BECAUSE GOD TOOK HIM AWAY.
—Gen. 5:23-24

I WOULD RATHER CREATE AN OUNCE OF HELP
THAN A TON OF THEORY.
—C. H. Spurgeon

SERVING GOD

If serving the LORD seems undesirable to you, then choose for yourselves this day whom you will serve, whether the gods your forefathers served beyond the River, or the gods of the Amorites, in whose land you are living. But as for me and my household, we will serve the LORD.
—Josh. 24:15

After 40 long years leading the Israelites in their desert wanderings, Moses prepared to die. On his deathbed, Moses passed the reins to Joshua, his capable assistant who many years before had given an inspiring report of what he saw in Canaan. Joshua had faithfully served God and helped lead His people through their desert wanderings. They were now poised on Canaan's border, ready to enter.

But there was a problem. The people preparing to possess Canaan had been born in the desert during the wandering years. They had never been to Egypt. They were never slaves. They had only heard of the great captivity and exodus. Wandering the desert was the only life they had known. While they had enjoyed many blessings and miracles from God's hand over the past 40 years, their spiritual lives were anemic, and they were chronic complainers. Joshua had his hands full.

Despite these challenges, Joshua continued trusting in God. The people claimed the Promised Land, defeated their enemies in God's strength, and settled down in rest to live in and enjoy the land of plenty given them by God. As the families grew and prospered, Joshua noticed a disturbing spiritual trend. The Israelites became self-sufficient. They began to believe they had accomplished all these wonderful blessings through their own strength and ingenuity. They had done it on their own—*their* way. Idols from their neighbors began to show up in their homes. They turned from God.

At the age of 110, Joshua assembled the people in a great revival service at Shechem, where they renewed their devotion and commitment to the Lord. But Joshua knew how fickle their hearts were and threw out the mighty challenge in today's verse.

In a day of plenty, when we have more than any generation before us, many still worship other gods rather than the God who has provided us with all we enjoy. As Sunday School teachers, let's echo Joshua's great challenge to our classes. Encourage your class to remember the source of all that is good and serve Him.

Prayer: *Lord, all that we have and all that we are we owe wholly to you and your unfathomable love and mercy for us. May we never forget that it all comes from your hand. Help us be like Joshua in our love and gratitude to you. In Jesus' name we pray. Amen.*

BLESSED ARE THEY WHOSE WAYS ARE BLAMELESS, WHO
WALK ACCORDING TO THE LAW OF THE LORD.
—Ps. 119:1

MUCH OF OUR DIFFICULTY AS SEEKING CHRISTIANS
STEMS FROM OUR UNWILLINGNESS TO TAKE GOD AS
HE IS AND ADJUST OUR LIVES ACCORDINGLY. WE
INSIST UPON TRYING TO MODIFY HIM AND BRING
HIM NEARER TO OUR OWN IMAGE.
—A. W. Tozer

DOING IT GOD'S WAY

*Aaron's sons Nadab and Abihu took their censers, put fire in them
and added incense; and they offered unauthorized fire before the LORD,
contrary to his command.*
—Lev. 10:1

*J*ust weeks after delivering the Israelites from their Egyptian captivity, God laid out for Moses a very organized and detailed plan of how He would deal with His people in spiritual matters. God's instructions about every aspect of worship, sacrifice, and prayer were meticulously exacting. God designed even the fabrics and colors of the Tabernacle materials along with the priests' clothing. Over and over, He reminded Moses to build everything precisely as He directed.

Why all the attention to such detail? Why the slavish devotion to so many precise procedures and obscure rituals? Before the foundation of the world, God planned how He would save His creation from their sins. His plan culminated in the life, death, resurrection, and ascension of His Son, Jesus. Until the Incarnation, God was teaching His people, training them, and preparing them for the eventual arrival of His Son. Every detail of worship and sacrifice and praise in the Old Testament points to Christ—the only Way to God.

So how did God react when His people did not follow His directions in their worship? Two of Aaron's sons found out the hard way.

Just in front of the heavy curtain separating the Holy Place from the holy of holies was the altar of incense. Each morning and evening the priest on duty tending the lamp was to burn fragrant incense whose specific recipe God had prescribed. The burning fragrance was to be a sweet savor to the Lord in worship.

Despite God's clear instructions and directions about how the altar of incense was to be tended, Nadab and Abihu offered the fire and incense to God in an unauthorized manner. While we don't know exactly what the brothers did wrong, God did. His fire consumed them on the spot for their disobedience.

In our day of relativism and often hazy interpretation of the Bible, such specific and swift punishment for what seems to be a minor procedural infraction is shocking to us. Yet it is a vivid reminder that God means what He says. We have a solemn duty to teach our Sunday School classes about God's high expectations for obedience while we are also speaking of His mercy and grace. A life of discipleship is built upon the perfect obedience modeled by Jesus.

God's standard of holiness is perfection, a standard we are completely unable to achieve on our own. With His commands come His enablements. Let's remind our classes that through Jesus Christ we can be forgiven our sins and made perfect in His likeness. He is the only way to gain access to God.

Prayer: *Father, we are painfully aware of our imperfections and inability on our own to attain the perfection you demand. We claim the blood and provision of Jesus Christ as our Savior to satisfy your justice and holiness. Give us the strength and desire to be obedient to your calling. In Jesus' name we pray. Amen.*

IN ALL YOUR WAYS ACKNOWLEDGE HIM,
AND HE WILL MAKE YOUR PATHS STRAIGHT.

—Prov. 3:6

FOR GOD TO EXPLAIN A TRIAL WOULD BE TO
DESTROY ITS PURPOSES, CALLING FORTH
SIMPLE FAITH AND IMPLICIT OBEDIENCE.

—Alfred Edersheim

GOD WANTS OUR CHOICEST AND BEST

God said, "Take your son, your only son, Isaac, whom you love,
and go to the region of Moriah. Sacrifice him there as a burnt offering
on one of the mountains I will tell you about."
—Gen. 22:2

What's the longest time you've ever had to wait for someone to keep a promise he or she made to you? A week? A month? A year?

Try 25 years!

When Abraham was 75 years old, God made him a seven-part promise. Promise number one was that Abraham would father a great nation of people who would outnumber the sands on the seashore. There were only two problems with God's promise: Abraham was 75, and his 65-year-old wife, Sarah, could not have children.

Twenty-five years after making the promises, God delivered—and so did Sarah. Abraham was 100, and Sarah was 90 when Isaac, the son of God's promise, was born. How the old couple cherished the boy for whom they had waited so long! They watched him grow into early manhood and centered their lives on his. Just when Abraham knew he was on the way to being the father of a great nation, God came calling again—and the promise seemed in dire jeopardy.

Scripture tells us God tested Abraham. He told the proud father to take his only son to a mountain three days away and offer him as a sacrifice to God. For most of us, such a command—even from God—would bring down a torrent of tears and complaints. "How could you make me wait 25 years for this promised boy, let him grow up, and now you want me to sacrifice him? He is the most precious person in the world to us. How could you do this?" Precisely, there's the rub.

Abraham was a man known for his faith and prompt obedience. He left with Isaac the very next day. Three days later, with Isaac bound on the altar, Abraham raised his knife to sacrifice the boy to the Lord. At that moment the angel of the Lord called out a restraining word to the old man. Abraham passed the test. God was still number one in the patriarch's life, and his actions proved his faith beyond any doubt.

This is the faith God rewards. Do our choicest and best possessions really belong to God? Is He really first in all parts of our lives? James was right: "I will show you my faith by what I do" (James 2:18). Do your actions show a watching Sunday School class that Jesus is Lord of your life? Hold your life and the things of value loosely. God will someday ask for them.

Prayer: *Dear Lord, you gave your best for me. Help me to honor you with everything I possess and everything I seek to do. May I ever place you before anything and everything I hold dear. In Jesus' name I pray. Amen.*

SEEK THE LORD WHILE HE MAY BE FOUND;
CALL ON HIM WHILE HE IS NEAR.

—Isa. 55:6

GOD'S WOUNDS CURE; SIN'S KISSES KILL.

—William Gurnall

"WHERE ARE YOU?"

The LORD God called to the man, "Where are you?"
—Gen. 3:9

*H*ave you ever closed your eyes and tried to imagine what living in the Garden of Eden was like for Adam and Eve? The most wondrous part of this life had to be the daily walks and talks with God. Just think—spending every afternoon with God in personal fellowship.

Through Adam and Eve's disobedience and sin, this fellowship was interrupted. What used to be a time of anticipation and joyful communion now became a time of dread and self-consciousness about their nakedness. Sin had opened their eyes, and they were ashamed to see God. The first thing they tried to do is what all sinners have done every day since that fateful day in the garden—they hid from God.

What about God? What was the first thing He did when Adam and Eve sinned? Did He wring His hands in anguish and have second thoughts about what He had created? Did He abandon His disobedient creation and throw up His hands in disgust?

Hardly. When Adam and Eve sinned, the first thing God did was come looking for them. Can you fathom the love He displayed in that simple question, "Where are you?" Make no mistake: God knew where they were physically and spiritually at that moment. And He still came looking for them.

Every moment since that awful day, God has continued to look for men and women, boys and girls, to save. The Old

Testament is one long history of God's dealing with His people in preparation for the coming of Jesus. Christ's life, death, resurrection, and ascension at last provided the one and only sure way through which sinful humanity can be reconciled with its holy Creator. Now God could point to His Son and say, "Here is the way to Me."

Each week, do you hold up before your Sunday School class a seeking Father who loves His creation so much He sacrificed His own Son that sinners might now have a way to become God's children? He still asks, "Where are you?" Does your class know this unfathomable truth?

Prayer: *Dear God, forgive us for trying to hide from you in our times of sin or disobedience. Help us to seek your face in prayer and stay constantly sensitive to your Holy Spirit's moving in our lives. In Christ's name. Amen.*

ON THE CONTRARY, WE SPEAK AS MEN APPROVED
BY GOD TO BE ENTRUSTED WITH THE GOSPEL.
WE ARE NOT TRYING TO PLEASE MEN BUT GOD,
WHO TESTS OUR HEARTS.
—1 Thess. 2:4

OBEDIENCE MEANS THAT I HAVE BANKED
EVERYTHING ON THE ATONEMENT, AND MY
OBEDIENCE IS MET IMMEDIATELY BY THE DELIGHT
OF THE SUPERNATURAL GRACE OF GOD.
—Oswald Chambers

GOD'S SPECIFIC CALL

At the LORD's command through Moses, each was assigned his work and told what to carry. Thus they were counted, as the LORD commanded Moses.
—Num. 4:49

When it comes to your spiritual life, did you know God called you to be a fluorescent tube and a laser beam?

All believers are called to be witnesses for Christ and to represent Him and the gospel in the broad arena in which we live and work. We're like strong fluorescent tubes—bright lights, softly illuminating a large area. We shed the light of the gospel in the circle of influence and acquaintances where we live and spend our time.

But we also have a smaller circle of friends, loved ones, and spiritual family—those with whom we spend more intense, good-quality time. Within this closer-knit community, we are to do and be much more than fluorescent lights of the gospel. We are to be powerful laser beams around these people on whose lives we exert powerful and eternal influence.

Lasers are tightly focused bundles of light, the power of which has been magnified so greatly that the light beam alone can slice through steel as if it's hot butter. They can be devastatingly dangerous weapons of destruction. In the deft hands of a skilled surgeon, lasers can cleanly cut away diseased tissue, restoring sight to the visually impaired and removing diseased tissue from the terminally ill.

God called all Levite men between the ages of 30 and 50 to be the keepers and priests of the Tabernacle. When it came time to move the camp and Tabernacle, there were three clans of Levites who took off their serving garments to perform their minutely specific roles in moving the holy things of God. Aaron and his family disassembled the Tabernacle and loaded the furnishings and serving pieces, including the ark, on carts pushed by the Kohathites. The Gershonites carried the many curtains, coverings, and connecting ropes. The Merarites shouldered the Tabernacle's frames, crossbars, posts, sockets, tent pegs, and support ropes. No one else could help the three clans in their duties. When moving day arrived, each clan had a specific call.

We Sunday School teachers have our general duties and places of service and daily witness, to be sure. But we have a specific call, too, when it comes to our classes. God has given us a specific responsibility—a laserlike duty of sharing God's Word—to perform every week. Although others can pray for us and lend support and counsel, only we can fulfill our call. We are both fluorescent tubes and laser beams for Christ. We are priests and servers with a very specific call as Sunday School teachers. May we be faithful.

Prayer: *Dear Father, what a privilege and honor we enjoy to be light reflecting your holiness and the call of salvation! May we be faithful to honor your will and design for our lives and ministry for you. In Jesus' name we pray. Amen.*

THE LORD SAID TO SAMUEL, "DO NOT CONSIDER HIS APPEARANCE OR HIS HEIGHT, FOR I HAVE REJECTED HIM. THE LORD DOES NOT LOOK AT THE THINGS MAN LOOKS AT. MAN LOOKS AT THE OUTWARD APPEARANCE, BUT THE LORD LOOKS AT THE HEART."
—1 Sam. 16:7

I AM NOT WHAT I OUGHT TO BE. I AM NOT WHAT I WANT TO BE. I AM NOT WHAT I HOPE TO BE. BUT STILL, I AM NOT WHAT I USED TO BE. AND BY THE GRACE OF GOD, I AM WHAT I AM.
—John Newton

THE MAN OF A DIFFERENT SPIRIT

Because my servant Caleb has a different spirit and follows me wholeheartedly, I will bring him into the land he went to, and his descendants will inherit it.
—Num. 14:24

Leading a Sunday School class can often make you feel much the way Moses must have felt not long after the 12 spies returned from their mission over in Canaan. Picture the scene. Hundreds of thousands of travel-weary people gathered around Moses and the spies, anxiously hanging onto every word of their report from inside the Promised Land. *Are we there yet? Is it ours? What does it look like? Is the soil fertile? Anyone else living there? Where's my plot of land? Can we go now?*

In their moment of anticipation, the report must have hit the Israelites like a plate of two-day-old manna! The good news is that the land is really flowing with milk and honey. Look at these grapes! The bad news is that the land is full of giants—huge, awful guys with terrible manners and no inter-

24

est in sharing the land with us. If we want the land, we'll have to fight these giants for it. Ten of the spies said, "We'll never be able to win." Joshua and Caleb said, "You're right, we won't—but *God* will. It's His land, and He gave it to us. Pack up your stuff, and let's move in."

The Israelites complained bitterly. They wanted to go back to Egypt. They wanted another leader. God's new adventure wasn't what they had expected. They even threatened to stone Moses!

Angered at their rebelliousness and disbelief, God promised that no Israelite over 20 years old would ever see any part of the Promised Land. For the next 40 years, the people were reduced to wandering aimlessly about the desert until all those who had disbelieved God's promise had died.

But God exempted one man in particular from His anger. Caleb was different from the others. He followed God wholeheartedly and was not the least bit frightened to claim God's promise and move up into Canaan. He believed God. He was obedient. His entire heart was wrapped up in pleasing God. He was God's servant. In short, he was a man of a different spirit. His love for God evoked a divine promise of future inheritance and blessing.

When your class becomes impossible and unruly, when everything seems to be going against you—even if they threaten to toss you out, have a heart like Caleb's. Be obedient. Serve God wholeheartedly. Be a teacher with a different spirit. God will reward your obedience just as He did Caleb's.

Prayer: *Dear Father, thank you for the opportunity and honor of leading this Sunday School class. Though the class can often be difficult, I know this is where you want me to be serving you. Give me a different spirit—like Caleb's—that I may serve you with all my heart. In Jesus' name I pray. Amen.*

GO AND PROCLAIM IN THE HEARING OF JERUSALEM:
"I REMEMBER THE DEVOTION OF YOUR YOUTH,
HOW AS A BRIDE YOU LOVED ME AND FOLLOWED
ME THROUGH THE DESERT, THROUGH
A LAND NOT SOWN."
—Jer. 2:2

WHATSOEVER WE HAVE OVER-LOVED, IDOLIZED,
AND LEANED UPON, GOD HAS FROM TIME TO TIME
BROKEN IT, AND MADE US TO SEE THE VANITY OF IT;
SO THAT WE FIND THE READIEST COURSE TO BE
RID OF OUR COMFORTS IS TO SET OUR HEARTS
INORDINATELY UPON THEM.
—John Flavel

DEVOTION TO GOD

The LORD said to Moses, "Make a snake and put it up on a pole;
anyone who is bitten can look at it and live."
—Num. 21:8

History gives us very little evidence that people generally learn from their experiences and change. After nearly 40 years wandering about in the desert as their punishment for disobedience, the new generation of Israelites behaved just as disobediently as their parents.

When they complained about the desert food, God sent manna. The people tired of this heavenly food and complained about not having any meat. God literally covered them up in quail. They complained about not having bread or water. They didn't like the route Moses was taking to the Promised Land. In general, there was nothing much they liked, so they picked on Moses and complained about his leadership.

Because of their disobedient attitudes and obstinate behavior, God sent venomous snakes among the people, and many Israelites died from snakebites as punishment. In fear for their lives, the people cried out for forgiveness. In mercy, God had Moses fashion a bronze snake atop a long pole placed in the center of camp. Whoever would simply look at the snake would be cured of their snakebites. Jesus relied on this event in describing His own ministry (John 3:14-15).

But a curious thing happened. After the deadly snakes were gone, after the move into the Promised Land, after almost 700 years as a nation, the bronze snake reappeared in Israelite history. King Hezekiah had just come to Judah's throne and was turning the wicked nation back to God. Among the idols and relics of idolatry Hezekiah destroyed was a bronze snake. You guessed it—the same bronze snake from the desert episode. By now the snake had been given a name and was being worshiped (2 Kings 18:4). The people had turned God's means of healing into a god to be worshiped. God richly rewarded the good king's obedience and righteousness in destroying it.

When it seems your preparation and teaching are yielding no fruit and some in your class keep returning to old sinful ways, remain devoted to God. Don't lose sight of His holiness and your high calling. He rewarded Hezekiah's obedience against all odds. He will take care of you too. Remain devoted to Him and His calling.

Prayer: *Dear God, while others may often return to their sinful ways and disregard everything I share with them from your Word, please keep me devoted to you and your will. Give me Hezekiah's devotion to you and his love for your ways. In Christ's name I pray. Amen.*

LISTEN TO ADVICE AND ACCEPT INSTRUCTION,
AND IN THE END YOU WILL BE WISE.

—Prov. 19:20

GOD'S WORK DONE GOD'S WAY WILL
NEVER LACK GOD'S SUPPLY.

—Hudson Taylor

THE FAITHFUL
FATHER-IN-LAW

Moses listened to his father-in-law and did everything he said.
—Exod. 18:24

*P*icture this scene in your mind: A tent without air conditioning in the middle of a blistering desert. Surrounding the tent is a couple million just-released slaves from Egypt and all their livestock milling around, awaiting a word from Moses on when the hike to the Promised Land will start. Between the heat, the scarcity of provisions, and the crowded conditions, tempers flare and nerves fray. When disagreements get out of hand, the people run to Moses to have him mediate.

Every day Moses sits at the door of this tent from sunup till sundown all by himself settling arguments and disputes. The disputants form an endless line from his doorway off to the horizon. He is weary beyond belief, and the people are worn out from waiting.

How big a job did Moses really have? Let's see—assume for a moment that all the women and the children in the camp got along famously. Assume there were 500,000 men and that half of these never argued with anybody. Suppose the other 250,000 men were each in some sort of argument with one other man. If Moses gave each of these 125,000 pairs of fighting men a five-minute hearing, it would take him 145 weeks—almost three years—working six days a week, 12 hours a day, just to process the people standing in line. That is if we make the assumption that no new fights broke out while Moses was trying to mediate the ones in line. Moses was in over his head.

No wonder Moses' father-in-law, Jethro, a godly man, was so shocked when he came to visit. The people were at their wits' end, and Moses was exhausted. After a thorough scolding, Jethro pulled Moses aside and suggested a simple but brilliant plan: divide the people and the work among capable men who can hear and decide the simple disagreements. Moses could hear the difficult ones. Everyone would share the pain and the gain. It's likely Moses had to identify and appoint about 65,000 men to implement Jethro's plan!

Teacher, don't try to do it all alone. Prayerfully select capable people in your class to take on the many duties and activities needed for a class to run efficiently. Let others share in the responsibility of ministry. Let them grow and mature in service. Challenge your class members to pray about getting involved in something that suits their talents. Moses divided God's people into groups of 1,000, 100, 50, and 10 and put a capable manager over each group. Each manager needed different skills given the size of their groups. The same is true for your class. Just as the people went home satisfied after Jethro's plan was implemented, so God will bless the work of your class leaders and bring glory to His name.

Prayer: *Dear Lord, please destroy in me the desire to do it all. I simply can't do it all. Give me the wisdom and courage to challenge my class to prayerfully accept their responsibilities in service to you and your kingdom. In Jesus' name I pray. Amen.*

I THANK MY GOD EVERY TIME I REMEMBER YOU.
—Phil. 1:3

WRITE YOUR PLANS IN PENCIL,
BUT GIVE GOD THE ERASER.
—Anonymous

HAVE YOU LEFT A MARKER?

*Each of you is to take up a stone on his shoulder, according to the number
of the tribes of the Israelites, to serve as a sign among you. In the future,
when your children ask you, "What do these stones mean?" tell them that the
flow of the Jordan was cut off before the ark of the covenant of the LORD.
When it crossed the Jordan, the waters of the Jordan were cut off.
These stones are to be a memorial to the people of Israel forever.*
—Josh. 4:5-7

How terribly short our memories can often be! We forget to stop at the store on the way home from work. We overlook an important birthday or anniversary. We lose the impact from an important life-changing event through forgetfulness. Our memories are simply not to be trusted. Many of us recognize this shortcoming. We make lists or program our PDAs or leave sticky notes on the steering wheel so we won't forget. The limits of human memory are why your credit card number is broken into four groups of four numbers each. Four is the optimal number of digits the human brain can easily recall.

For the really important things in life we go out of our way to remember. We build monuments or erect structures to commemorate people and events. We take our children to these places, and the monuments help to preserve the important memory. If you've ever visited the Pearl Harbor Memorial or worshiped in Chicago's historic Moody Church, you'll never forget the experience.

Just so future generations would never forget how God had led their forebears up out of the desert into the Promised Land, God instructed Joshua to have one man from each of the 12 tribes take up a large stone out of the flooding Jordan's dry bed and erect an altar on the shore. This altar served as a reminder to future generations of God's great hand of deliverance. In years to come, when children saw the pile of stones and asked about them, the rocks would be an object lesson so the people would never forget what God did for them.

Have you erected any remembrances to God for your class to see? When they hear a specific verse of Scripture or see your life or hear about your favorite missionary, do they remember Christ? Do any of these things trigger their memories of hearing you proclaiming the good news of the gospel? What stones have you stacked up to remind future generations of what God has done in your life and ministry?

Prayer: *Dear Father, how great and memorable are your ways and your gracious provision for us in our times of need! May we always recall and cherish your help and support. In Jesus' name we pray. Amen.*

SUBMIT YOURSELVES, THEN, TO GOD. RESIST THE
DEVIL, AND HE WILL FLEE FROM YOU.
—James 4:7

DON'T PRAY TO ESCAPE TROUBLE. DON'T PRAY
TO BE COMFORTABLE IN YOUR EMOTIONS.
PRAY TO DO THE WILL OF GOD IN EVERY SITUATION.
NOTHING ELSE IS WORTH PRAYING FOR.
—Samuel M. Shoemaker

BEING WHERE YOU'RE SUPPOSED TO BE

In the spring, at the time when kings go off to war, David sent Joab out with the king's men and the whole Israelite army. They destroyed the Ammonites and besieged Rabbah. But David remained in Jerusalem.
—2 Sam. 11:1

Most of us operate on a schedule of some sort since other people rely on us. Almost every vocation or job requires that we be in certain places at certain times routinely. Every Sunday at set times we expect our pastor to be in the pulpit. During business hours, we expect our banker or our doctor or our auto mechanic to be in the office or shop. Should we dial 911 in an emergency, we expect a competent human to answer on the first ring. Life simply requires attendance at certain times.

When we're not where we're supposed to be when we're supposed to be there, disappointing and even dangerous things can happen. Your imagination can easily paint all sorts of dreadful pictures when obligations are not met.

In Old Testament times, springtime weather conditions were optimal for conducting warfare. After 10 years on the throne, David and his armies had just about conquered God's enemies—but not all of them. For reasons known only to

David and God, the spring season in our verse found David at home, where he wasn't supposed to be. He sent general Joab out to lead God's army, but King David should have been at the helm. He was home alone, at ease.

The rest is history. That one decision to stay home that particular springtime put into motion a series of events that devastated David and his family for generations to come. What heartache followed when David failed to be where he was expected to be! His life and the history of Israel were altered forever.

Do you have a burning desire to always meet your obligations? Is being where you're supposed to be when you're supposed to be there one of your top priorities? Can your Sunday School class always depend on you to be there for them? Our Lord is the perfect example of dependability. Are you following in His steps?

Prayer: *Dear God, you know all the activities and people who compete for my limited time and resources. Please give me the strength and wisdom to fulfill my commitments always and to be where I am supposed to be in your service. In Christ's name I pray. Amen.*

DEAR FRIENDS, NOW WE ARE CHILDREN OF GOD, AND
WHAT WE WILL BE HAS NOT YET BEEN MADE KNOWN.
BUT WE KNOW THAT WHEN HE APPEARS, WE SHALL BE
LIKE HIM, FOR WE SHALL SEE HIM AS HE IS.

—1 John 3:2

THE MOST SPIRITUAL AND SANCTIFIED MINDS, WHEN
THEY FULLY PERCEIVE THE MAJESTY AND HOLINESS OF
GOD, ARE SO GREATLY CONSCIOUS OF THE GREAT
DISPROPORTION BETWEEN THEMSELVES AND THE LORD
THAT THEY ARE HUMBLED AND FILLED WITH HOLY
AWE, AND EVEN WITH DREAD AND ALARM.

—C. H. Spurgeon

WHAT'S YOUR
VIEW OF GOD?

*"Woe to me!" I cried. "I am ruined! For I am a man of unclean lips, and I live
among a people of unclean lips, and my eyes have seen the King, the LORD
Almighty."*
—Isa. 6:5

Our view of God sets the basis for every other belief we have.
If we consider God to be some doting, generous, and soft-
hearted grandfather figure smiling down on us, our lives and
the way we live will reflect that notion. The general spiritual
condition of our society today can be traced largely to an anemic opinion of God. One of the reasons sin is so rampant today is because so many people see only God's love, mercy, and
kindness. They don't view Him in *all* His attributes.

It's very clear that Isaiah did not hold an anemic view of
God. Some people suffer from a "moon view" of God. They
see a fraction of His attributes and think that's all there is to

God. That's similar to seeing the moon in quarter phase and thinking that's the entire moon.

God is often viewed as a dispenser of gifts, existing solely to meet our "felt needs"; someone who is there at our beck and call just to make us happy and feel fulfilled.

But there's another facet of God, and Isaiah saw it clearly. The prophet witnessed firsthand God's incredible holiness and righteousness—a holiness that is beyond our comprehension. Isaiah saw it and was terrified at his own sinfulness. When his life was viewed in the light of God's holiness, Isaiah saw his own uncleanness and wanted only to hide from God's blazing presence.

Which phase of the moon do we project to our Sunday School classes? Do we only speak of God's "love" side, or do we declare the full glory of all God's attributes, including His holiness? This side of God is bathed in justice, holiness, and righteousness. His wrath at sin and ungodliness is frightful, beyond imagination. He condemns sinners to an eternal hell. This side of God is real—just as real as His love and mercy.

As declarers of God's Word, we are responsible to show all of God as He is displayed in His Word. Don't shortchange your class by telling them only what they want to hear about God. Declare to them the full-orbed truth of God. Let Him work His message into our hearts.

Prayer: *Dear Father, we are appalled at our sinfulness and unworthiness when we try to see ourselves through your holy eyes. Remind us of your love and forgiveness, yet let us always consider and meditate on your holiness and righteousness. In Jesus' name we pray. Amen.*

TO THE WICKED, GOD SAYS: "WHAT RIGHT
HAVE YOU TO RECITE MY LAWS OR
TAKE MY COVENANT ON YOUR LIPS?"
—Ps. 50:16

WHAT IS GOD'S REMEDY FOR DEJECTION AT APPARENT
FAILURE IN OUR LABOURS? THIS—THE ASSURANCE
THAT GOD'S PURPOSE CANNOT FAIL, THAT GOD'S
PLANS CANNOT MISCARRY, THAT GOD'S WILL MUST BE
DONE. OUR LABOURS ARE NOT INTENDED TO BRING
ABOUT THAT WHICH GOD HAS NOT DECREED.
—Arthur W. Pink

GOD'S DEPARTING GLORY

*Then the glory of the LORD departed from over the threshold of the temple
and stopped above the cherubim. While I watched, the cherubim spread their
wings and rose from the ground, and as they went, the wheels went with
them. They stopped at the entrance to the east gate of the LORD's house,
and the glory of the God of Israel was above them.*
—Ezek. 10:18-19

Ezekiel's vision is indeed one of the most unusual and diffi-
cult-to-interpret stories in all of Scripture. Yet in the midst
of spinning wheels, flashing lights, and heavenly beings,
Ezekiel saw one thing that comes through with unmistakable
clarity: God's hatred of wickedness and sin among His people.

Israel's sin and idolatry had grown so greatly that God
could no longer tolerate what He saw. He intervened in the
history of His people and began to mete out justice, especially
to those in political and spiritual leadership over the country.

God's judgment reached its pinnacle when He began to
withdraw His glory from the Temple. From the days of the
Tabernacle in the desert, God had always met with His people
between the outstretched wings of the solid gold cherubim

covering the mercy seat atop the ark of the covenant. Annually on the Day of Atonement, the chief priest was permitted to offer a blood sacrifice for the people in God's presence before the ark in the holy of holies. This was the only means of national salvation until Jesus came.

For God to withdraw His presence from His people surely signaled an inconceivably dreadful spiritual situation. While we live under the new covenant and have ready access to God, we must always remember that He will not dwell where sin has taken up residence. Our Sunday School classes must know of God's holiness and His hatred of sin. Always encourage them to remain sensitive to the Holy Spirit's conviction, always desiring to be open and transparent to God's holy inspection. May we never become so hard and rebellious that God stops dealing with us.

Prayer: *Dear Heavenly Father, we shudder to think of how terrible it would be like for your Spirit to leave us. May we always remain sensitive to your moving in our hearts and ever seek to be obedient to your leading. In Christ's name we pray. Amen.*

CAST ALL YOUR ANXIETY ON HIM
BECAUSE HE CARES FOR YOU.
—1 Pet. 5:7

THE GREAT HINDRANCE IN SPIRITUAL LIFE IS THAT WE
WILL LOOK FOR BIG THINGS TO DO. "JESUS TOOK A
TOWEL . . . AND BEGAN TO WASH THE DISCIPLES' FEET."
—Oswald Chambers

GOD'S CALL TO DO THE IMPOSSIBLE

When the LORD began to speak through Hosea, the LORD said to him, "Go, take to yourself an adulterous wife and children of unfaithfulness, because the land is guilty of the vilest adultery in departing from the LORD." So he married Gomer daughter of Diblaim, and she conceived and bore him a son.
—Hos. 1:2-3

There's a part of all of us Sunday School teachers that's just dying for the Lord to call us to some grand, spectacular feat of spiritual accomplishment. We want a modern-day version of Elijah's nationally publicized, electrically charged victory over the forces of Satan and evil atop Mount Carmel. We naturally want to do great things for God—*big* things.

What happens when God asks us to do something quite unspectacular, even downright detestable, in our opinion? Consider a man named Hosea, one of God's prophets who lived just after the prophet Amos. Israel's sinfulness and disobedience were so great that God called on Amos to threaten His judgment at the hands of an unnamed enemy. Hosea followed and likewise proclaimed God's message to the disobedient Israelites for 38 years—without results.

To graphically show the people how far they had wandered, God made a public example of the well-known prophet. He told Hosea to marry an adulterous woman who had children fathered by her adulterous partners. Hosea was obedient, and his story is one of indescribable pain and agony. No surprise. Gomer continued her adulterous ways throughout their marriage, just as Israel continued in its idolatrous affairs against God. In the end, Hosea had to buy Gomer off the public auction block, where her life of sin had landed her in shame, nakedness, and disgrace. Her life had spiraled out of control as Hosea reached out to her in love at every turn.

Through Hosea, God showed His great love to His people. Even though they were an adulterous people living in continuous disobedience, God's love reached out to them time and again until at last He purchased all of sinful humanity off the auction block at the price of His only Son.

How did God show the people their terrible sin and His infinite love? He called one of His own prophets to do an unthinkably detestable thing, but Hosea was obedient, and God's name was glorified.

Has God laid an impossible family or child on your heart? Has He asked you to show His great love to someone else—someone who is impossibly unlovable? Would you rather be conquering mighty foes than ministering by example to the unlovable? Be obedient. Trust the Lord's wisdom. Like Hosea, God will bring glory to His name through your obedience in doing what you might consider an impossible thing.

Prayer: *Dear Lord, it seems that so many of us want to do great things for you when you are calling us rather to be faithful and obedient. Give us the strength and wisdom to be obedient to your call no matter what our thoughts may be. In your Son's name we pray. Amen.*

WE MUST PAY MORE CAREFUL ATTENTION,
THEREFORE, TO WHAT WE HAVE HEARD,
SO THAT WE DO NOT DRIFT AWAY.
—Heb. 2:1

LIVE AS THOUGH CHRIST DIED YESTERDAY,
ROSE FROM THE GRAVE TODAY,
AND IS COMING BACK TOMORROW.
—Theodore Epp

BECOMING AN EFFECTIVE WATCHMAN

*If the watchman sees the sword coming and does not blow the trumpet to
warn the people and the sword comes and takes the life of one of them,
that man will be taken away because of his sin, but I will hold
the watchman accountable for his blood. Son of man,
I have made you a watchman for the house of Israel.*
—Ezek. 33:6-7

Talk about a no-win job! Try being a watchman atop the
wall of an Old Testament city. Forced to remain vigilant for
long hours under all sorts of weather conditions, he found it
easy to get worn down physically and emotionally. If you saw
the enemy and blew the warning trumpet, an enemy arrow
might get you from a distance. Or your comrades might ac-
cuse you of not reacting fast enough. If you saw the enemy
approaching but failed to blow your trumpet for whatever reason, you were held responsible for all the damage and death
brought by the enemy. It would all be on your head.

Knowing the upcoming final destruction of Israel, God
called Ezekiel to a quiet place and appointed the prophet as
watchman over His people. Ezekiel was to preach repentance
and restoration to the Israelites. The symbolism of his call was
not lost on the prophet. He obeyed God's instructions even

when promised that the people would not listen to his message. Imagine being made accountable for your nation's spiritual condition while being told they would not listen to your preaching.

We Sunday School teachers are a lot like Ezekiel. God has called each of us to be a watchman for our class. We are responsible for delivering God's Word to those whom He has entrusted to our care. We see the evil in this world. From our experiences, we know the effects of sin. It is our duty to warn our classes and tell them of the disasters to come if they do not repent. While we are to be pillars of support and understanding to our classes, we are also to be voices of warning and direction. If we fail to do this, the potential spiritual wreckage of our classes could be on our heads.

So how do I become an effective watchman for my class like Ezekiel? Listen to God. Trust His call. Seek His guidance. Accept responsibility, and lean heavily on God for guidance, direction, and strength.

Prayer: *Dear God, thank you for calling me and enabling me to lead my Sunday School class. May I never forget the eternal consequences of my role as their spiritual watchman. Enable me through your Spirit to be diligent and watchful. In Jesus' name I pray. Amen.*

NO ONE KNOWS ABOUT THAT DAY OR HOUR,
NOT EVEN THE ANGELS IN HEAVEN, NOR THE SON,
BUT ONLY THE FATHER. BE ON GUARD! BE ALERT!
YOU DO NOT KNOW WHEN THAT TIME WILL COME.
—Mark 13:32-33

THERE IS ONLY ONE WAY TO DEVELOP AND GROW
SPIRITUALLY, AND THAT IS THROUGH FOCUSING
AND CONCENTRATING ON GOD.
—Oswald Chambers

A HEAVENLY MOTIVATION

I press on toward the goal to win the prize for
which God has called me heavenward in Christ Jesus.
—Phil. 3:14

Christianity demands discipline plus determination. Just as the runner who is not disciplined will lose the contest, so the believer who is not disciplined will not enjoy success. What was Paul's motivation for this disciplined life? It's found in Phil. 3:14.

Some scholars believe the phrase "high calling" refers to the day when believers will be caught away to be with Jesus Christ. Paul lived in the light of this grand future event. Paul looked for the coming of the Savior. This was one of the great motivations of his life. He literally lived in the glow and excitement of the return of Jesus Christ.

Some years ago former President Dwight D. Eisenhower was in the city of Denver. After attending morning worship in his wife's home church, he visited the home of a little boy who was stricken with cancer. The president came unannounced, went up to the little white frame house, and knocked at the door. The boy's father came to the door and, of course, was overwhelmed by whom he found there. He had been working around the house, and his hair was uncombed, his face unshaven. He was wearing an old T-shirt and torn blue jeans, and there stood President Eisenhower and his assistants.

The presidential party was ushered into the humble home, and a little gift was given to the boy. Eisenhower picked the little boy up in his arms and took him out to look at the limousine. In 15 minutes the group was gone. The whole neighborhood was buzzing and excited—that is, everyone was excited except the father. All he could think of was his uncombed hair, bearded face, dirty T-shirt, and torn blue jeans. What a way to meet the president of the United States!

One day Jesus Christ will come. Are you living in the excitement of the "upward calling"? May you approach your class with excitement and anticipation that Christ is not only present through His Holy Spirit but also will return. The apostle Paul lived in the glow of Christ's return. For a triumphant life, live with this heavenly motivation.

Prayer: *Lord, sometimes we are so focused on today's demands and duties that we forget our glorious future. Help me live in anticipation of your return. Help me to live with the hope of being with you for all eternity. In Jesus' name I pray. Amen.*

WE SENT TIMOTHY, WHO IS OUR BROTHER AND
GOD'S FELLOW WORKER IN SPREADING THE
GOSPEL OF CHRIST, TO STRENGTHEN
AND ENCOURAGE YOU IN YOUR FAITH.
—1 Thess. 3:2

GOD IS USING ME FROM HIS GREAT PERSPECTIVE,
AND ALL HE ASKS OF ME IS THAT I TRUST HIM.
—Oswald Chambers

A LEADERSHIP STYLE THAT WORKS

You know, brothers, that our visit to you was not a failure. We had previously suffered and been insulted in Philippi, as you know, but with the help of our God we dared to tell you his gospel in spite of strong opposition.
—1 Thess. 2:1-2

*I*f there is one ingredient that's essential to the success of an organization, it's leadership. Whether it's a business, church, athletic team, military unit, home, or whatever, the secret of progress usually rests with those who are in charge— the leaders.

Our world abounds with information on the subject of leadership. This data is communicated through films, videotapes, DVDs, CDs, cassette tapes, seminars, conferences, and books, all of which are designed to help us become better leaders. Sometimes the promises conveyed are true. However, more often than not we're simply left with another set of techniques leaving us frustrated and overwhelmed rather than free and confident. Furthermore, these numerous materials seldom take us to the Scriptures to discover what God has to say about leadership.

Today we want to depart from the norm and turn to God's Word for the direction we need.

Since leadership is so important, we need to be clear about what it is. One definition of leadership is "inspiring influence." Those who lead others with the greatest degree of success are able to light the spark, prompting others toward cooperation, hard work, and, if necessary, personal sacrifice. We should not assume there's only one style of leadership. Some people are hard-charging leaders who rely almost exclusively on extrinsic motivation. Others lead in a very laid-back and quiet fashion, never raising their voices above a conversational tone. Both styles can be equally effective and inspiring. Effective leaders can be found with all different temperaments. In fact, I believe all of us to some degree are leaders: at work, church, class, school; with family, friends, or someone with whom you have influence.

One key ingredient to being a successful leader is the ability to get along with people. A leader cannot be successful unless he or she can deal well with people. Over and above intelligence, decisiveness, job knowledge, and technical skills, no other factor makes as great a difference as this one.

Prayer: *Lord, show me how to share your truth with others. Help me to remember that I'm not adequately prepared to speak for you until I've spent personal time with you.*

I WILL GIVE YOU A NEW HEART AND PUT A NEW SPIRIT
IN YOU; I WILL REMOVE FROM YOU YOUR HEART OF
STONE AND GIVE YOU A HEART OF FLESH. AND I WILL
PUT MY SPIRIT IN YOU AND MOVE YOU TO FOLLOW
MY DECREES AND BE CAREFUL TO KEEP MY LAWS.
—Ezek. 36:26-27

RENEWING GRACE WORKS AS GREAT A CHANGE IN
THE SOUL AS THE TURNING A DEAD STONE INTO
LIVING FLESH. GOD WILL PUT HIS SPIRIT WITHIN,
AS A TEACHER, GUIDE, AND SANCTIFIER.
THE PROMISE OF GOD'S GRACE TO FIT US
FOR OUR DUTY SHOULD QUICKEN OUR CONSTANT
CARE AND ENDEAVOR TO DO OUR DUTY.
—Matthew Henry

A NEW HEART

"This is the covenant I will make with the house of Israel after that time," declares the LORD. "I will put my law in their minds and write it on their hearts. I will be their God, and they will be my people."
—Jer. 31:33

I've used many different tools to help improve my ability to remember names, appointments, calendar events, and special occasions. Among the tools used are Day Timers, Seven Habits Organizer, Franklin Planners, Jerry Lucas memory techniques, word association—and the list continues. Unless my calendar and planner are before me, I have a tendency to forget some things.

However, some things I don't have any trouble remembering. I've never forgotten a vacation, a day off work, my wedding anniversary, my wife's or children's birthdays, or Christmas. I've come to realize that I remember the things of the heart.

God, knowing our tendencies to forget, gives us a tremendous promise in Jer. 31:33.

If we're willing, God will put His laws in our minds and write them on our hearts. He'll help us remember His Word. He'll not only help us remember but also create a desire to obey His Word. Ask God to give you a hunger and thirst for His Word. As you study the Word, ask God to write it on your mind and heart. Ask Him to speak to you as you prepare to teach His Word. Ask Him to speak through you to the hearts and minds of your students. God's Word will purify, strengthen, and nourish the spiritual life of your students and you.

Prayer: *Lord, create in me a clean heart. Use me to share your Word with the students in my class and others with whom I come in contact.*

IF ANYONE IS IN CHRIST, HE IS A NEW CREATION;
THE OLD HAS GONE, THE NEW HAS COME!
—2 Cor. 5:17

THE BELIEVER IS CREATED ANEW; HIS HEART IS NOT
MERELY SET RIGHT, BUT A NEW HEART IS GIVEN HIM.
HE IS THE WORKMANSHIP OF GOD, CREATED IN
CHRIST JESUS UNTO GOOD WORKS.
—Matthew Henry

A REDESIGNED PERSON

*I consider everything a loss compared to the surpassing greatness of knowing
Christ Jesus my Lord, for whose sake I have lost all things. I consider them
rubbish, that I may gain Christ and be found in him, not having a
righteousness of my own that comes from the law, but that which is through
faith in Christ—the righteousness that comes from God and is by faith.*
—Phil. 3:8-9

Paul was one of the noblest characters in the ancient world. His biographical sketch at one time could have included an endless list of credentials and credits, which afforded him a host of privileges: power, position, and prestige. In Phil. 3:8-9, using imagery from business, Paul drew a picture of debits and credits. He said that everything once perceived to be listed in the debit column had been transferred to the credit column; what he once thought was profit was now loss. Things that once seemed so very important suddenly became extremely unimportant. People once thought of as influential and beneficial suddenly became noninfluential. Goals that once governed the entire direction of his life suddenly were redirected and channeled into completely different directions. What brought about this sudden 180? It was a personal, life-changing encounter with the Lord Jesus Christ.

Maybe you have experienced a similar change in your life. Maybe career plans have been reprioritized. Maybe an attitude has been reshaped. Maybe a habit has been discarded. When we experience the life-changing encounter with Christ, we find the bottom line of the ledger changes.

Paul's description of this change and the choice of words in these verses are interesting: rubbish/gain. In my mind, "rubbish" refers to something destined to be thrown away. I can't think of any better advice than to throw away, or cast aside, that which would beset us. Someone has suggested that the world is basically composed of two kinds of people: pitchers and savers—those who throw things away and those who hang on to things forever. When it comes to our spiritual lives, the correct strategy is to throw away the old way of life. When we throw away the old life, we gain the new; we receive the reoriented, reshaped, redesigned person God wants us to be.

Prayer: *Lord, I throw aside everything that would hinder me from being at my best for you. I surrender to your work in my life. Reorient, reshape, and redesign me into the person you desire.*

THAT IS WHY I AM SUFFERING AS I AM. YET I AM NOT ASHAMED, BECAUSE I KNOW WHOM I HAVE BELIEVED, AND AM CONVINCED THAT HE IS ABLE TO GUARD WHAT I HAVE ENTRUSTED TO HIM FOR THAT DAY.
—2 Tim. 1:12

GOD HAS NOT GIVEN US THE SPIRIT OF FEAR, BUT THE SPIRIT OF POWER, OF COURAGE AND RESOLUTION, TO MEET DIFFICULTIES AND DANGERS; THE SPIRIT OF LOVE TO HIM, WHICH WILL CARRY US THROUGH OPPOSITION.
—Matthew Henry

A SECURITY THAT'S ADEQUATE

Let your gentleness be evident to all. The Lord is near. Do not be anxious about anything, but in everything, by prayer and petition, with thanksgiving, present your requests to God.
—Phil. 4:5-6

Years ago under the Stalin regime a group of 30 Russian peasants met together secretly for worship. On one occasion their worship was interrupted by the arrival of Stalin's military police. The name of every person present was taken by the police. About the time the soldier was completing his task, one of the old men in the assembly piped up and said, "You forgot one." The soldier recounted the people and then compared that to the number of names he had gathered—both equaled 30. Still the old man persisted—"You forgot one." The soldier grew impatient, and when pressed to explain, the old man said, "There is one you have not recorded. The Lord Jesus Christ—He is here."

Paul reminds us of this truth in Phil. 4:5 that "the Lord is near." Paul skillfully inserts these words and in so doing conveys his confidence in the intimacy and adequacy of Christ's living presence through the Holy Spirit. I like the Phillips translation of this phrase: "Never forget the nearness of your Lord."

If we remember the nearness of the Lord, we need have no anxiety. We should heed Paul's pleas: "In every thing by prayer and supplication with thanksgiving let your requests be made known unto God" (v. 6, KJV).

Alexis Carrel, author of the *Man: The Unknown,* once wrote an article for *Reader's Digest* sharing his testimony:

As a physician, I have seen men after all other therapy had failed, lifted out of disease and melancholy by the serene effort of prayer. It is the power in the world that seems to overcome the so-called laws of nature. The occasions on which prayer has dramatically done this have been termed miracles. But a constant, quieter miracle takes place hourly in the hearts of men and women who have discovered that prayer supplies them with a steady flow of sustaining power in their daily lives."

Don't ever forget: The Lord is near!

Prayer: *Lord, I am filled with praise for your abiding presence. May my heart feel you. May my eyes see you. May my ears hear you speak. May I never forget that you are as close as the mention of your name. In Jesus' name I pray. Amen.*

I HAVE GIVEN YOU AUTHORITY TO TRAMPLE ON
SNAKES AND SCORPIONS AND TO OVERCOME ALL THE
POWER OF THE ENEMY; NOTHING WILL HARM YOU.
—Luke 10:19

THE MORE SIMPLY DEPENDENT WE ARE ON THE
TEACHING, HELP, AND BLESSING OF THE SON OF GOD,
THE MORE WE SHALL KNOW BOTH OF THE FATHER
AND OF THE SON; THE MORE BLESSED WE SHALL BE
IN SEEING THE GLORY, AND HEARING THE WORDS OF
THE DIVINE SAVIOUR; AND THE MORE USEFUL WE
SHALL BE MADE IN PROMOTING HIS CAUSE.
—Matthew Henry

A WAY OUT

*We have this treasure in jars of clay to show that this all-surpassing power
is from God and not from us. We are hard pressed on every side, but not
crushed; perplexed, but not in despair; persecuted, but not abandoned;
struck down, but not destroyed. We always carry around in our body the
death of Jesus, so that the life of Jesus may also be revealed in our body.
For we who are alive are always being given over to death for Jesus' sake,
so that his life may be revealed in our mortal body. So then,
death is at work in us, but life is at work in you.*
—2 Cor. 4:7-12

Have you ever been to a tennis tournament? It's fun to
watch the skills and talents of the players. It's also fun to
watch the crowd follow the ball from left to right. Back and
forth. Back and forth. Back and forth. In 2 Cor. 4:7-12, you
get that same feeling. Paul is volleying between trial and triumph. Trial and triumph. Trial and triumph. It's a fact you
and I are going to experience some tough days. We're also going to have triumph.

In verse 8 Paul said he was "pressed on every side."
"Pressed" is the word used for crushing grapes. Sometimes life

crushes down upon us, and we feel pressured, as in a vise. It's the feeling of a student in the middle of exam week or at the end of the semester or a teacher finishing up the semester with papers to grade. It's the feeling that your world is coming down as you grit your teeth and hold on.

We all experience pressures in our lives from finances, deadlines, and demands of friends and family. Paul says we're pressured and afflicted in every way, but not crushed. Even if we're in a difficult circumstance or situation, with God there's an escape route. Our extremity is God's opportunity. We're pressured but not totally so.

Don't forget that regardless of the pressures, trials, or temptations, God will make a way.

Prayer: *Lord, thank you for your wonderful promises. I rest in you, knowing that you're working in all of life's circumstances. I commit myself and my class to your care.*

WE DEALT WITH EACH OF YOU AS A FATHER DEALS
WITH HIS OWN CHILDREN, ENCOURAGING,
COMFORTING AND URGING YOU TO LIVE LIVES
WORTHY OF GOD, WHO CALLS YOU INTO
HIS KINGDOM AND GLORY.
—1 Thess. 2:11-12

REGARDLESS OF YOUR AGE, GOD CAN USE YOU.
TEACH WITH A DEVOTION TO GOD AND HIS WORD.
LIVE SO OTHERS CAN SEE CHRIST IN YOU.

AN OPEN LETTER

*Are we beginning to commend ourselves again? Or do we need, like some
people, letters of recommendation to you or from you? You yourselves are
our letter, written on our hearts, known and read by everybody. You show
that you are a letter from Christ, the result of our ministry, written not
with ink but with the Spirit of the living God, not on tablets of stone
but on tablets of human hearts.*
—2 Cor. 3:1-3

*P*aul referred to the custom that was common in the ancient
world of sending letters of commendation with a person. If
someone was going to a strange community, a friend who
knew someone in that community would give a letter of commendation to introduce the person and to testify to his or her
character. Here Paul declares that the only commendation he
needs is the Corinthians.

The change in their character and lives is his commendation. He goes on to make a great claim: every one of them is a
letter of Christ.

Long ago Plato said the good teacher does not write his or
her message in ink that will fade; rather, the message is written upon humanity. That's what Jesus has done. He wrote His
message on the Corinthians, through His servant Paul, not

with fading ink but with the Spirit, not on tablets of stone as the Law was first written, but on their hearts.

This is a great truth—every person is an open letter for Jesus Christ. Every Christian, whether we like it or not, is an advertisement for Christianity. The honor of Christ is in our hands. We judge a shopkeeper by the kind of goods sold; we judge a craftsman by the kind of articles produced; we judge a church by the kind of people it creates; we judge a Sunday School class by the kind of disciples it helps to form; and people judge Christ by His followers. When we go out into the world, we have the awe-inspiring responsibility of being advertisements for Christ and His Church.

Prayer: *Lord, your honor is in our hands. May your Holy Spirit enable and empower me to live such a godly life that others will see you. May I be a good representative of you in my world. In your Son's name I pray. Amen.*

AS IRON SHARPENS IRON,
SO ONE MAN SHARPENS ANOTHER.
—Prov. 27:17

TRUE FRIENDS BRING OUT THE BEST IN EACH OTHER.

BEING A FRIEND

Some people brought to him a man who was deaf and could hardly talk,
and they begged him to place his hand on the man.
—Mark 7:32

*D*avid Levenson wrote a book titled *The Seasons of a Man's Life*. In examination of the factors that contribute to the development, growth, and success of people, he discovered three primary factors that seem to be essential to success. The first is a great vision; a driving dream moves and motivates you to do something with your life. The second factor common to the successful people he studied was they each found a teacher who could instruct and help them along the way. The third commonality among these successful people was the deep personal and significant relationship with at least one other person—someone who would support them in accomplishing their dreams.

In Mark 7:32 we see a crippled man's friends who brought him to Jesus. His friends were determined to see that he got the help he needed. They cared enough about him to intervene in his behalf.

A few years ago *The Betty Ford Story* was aired on television, produced with the help of Betty Ford herself. The story dealt with her addiction to alcohol and prescription drugs. She was overwhelmed by the stress of being the first lady compounded by the debilitating pain of arthritis. These factors eventually led her to pain pills and finally alcohol addiction. Fortunately, her family loved her enough to confront her with her problems. In the most powerful scene of the movie, her family members share their love and concern for her one by one. They tell her she has become addicted to prescription medicine and is an alcoholic. At first, Betty denies her problem. But her persistent family continues to love her, and she eventually realizes she must seek help.

During the same scene, Susan, the youngest child, says to her, "Mother, always before when you had a problem, you turned to God and to your family, but lately you've shut us out. You've turned to medicine and drinking, and you're killing yourself." Susan was being not only a daughter but a friend as well.

When you see friends in trouble, you seek to intervene. You must make certain they get the help they need. So it was with the man whose friends brought him to see Jesus. They believed that Jesus could help him. In Sunday School you'll see people who have great needs. Your responsibility as a teacher is to help, support, lift, love, and bring them to Jesus. How wonderful it is to have friends like that! How wonderful it is to *be* a friend like that!

Prayer: *Lord, help me to be a real friend to those in my class. May I help, encourage, support, lift, and love them. May I also be strong enough to intervene and speak the truth in love when your Spirit directs me.*

SOME MEN CAME, BRINGING TO HIM A PARALYTIC,
CARRIED BY FOUR OF THEM.
—Mark 2:3

HUMAN NEED MOVED THESE FOUR MEN; LET IT ALSO
MOVE YOU TO COMPASSIONATE ACTION. WHEN YOU
RECOGNIZE SOMEONE'S NEED, DO YOU ACT?
—*Life Application Bible* notes

COOPERATION IN LIFE

*Whatever happens, conduct yourselves in a manner worthy of the gospel
of Christ. Then, whether I come and see you or only hear about you
in my absence, I will know that you stand firm in one spirit,
contending as one man for the faith of the gospel.*
—Phil. 1:27

I read a story of a lifeguard on a beach who heard a woman
cry for help. He swam out to the frantic woman and
grabbed her by the hair. He then swam back to shore, only to
discover that he had a wig in his hand. He swam back to the
woman and grabbed her arm and upon reaching the shore
saw he had brought back an artificial arm. He swam back out
again and grabbed a leg. You guessed it—it was an artificial
leg. He swam back out to the screaming woman and said,
"Woman, if you want to be saved from drowning, you had
better begin to cooperate with me!"

We get nowhere fast when we detach ourselves from others
and fail to unite our hearts and hands in cooperation. We really
do need each other. We can do more together than we can do
individually. In his book *The Seven Habits of Highly Effective People*, Stephen Covey introduced a new word to our vocabularies
and conversations: "synergy." The basic idea behind synergy is
that the whole is greater than the sum of all its parts. Synergy
takes place when two or more people together produce more
than the sum of what they could have produced separately.

As Sunday School teachers you're not called to be lone rangers. Allow other people and students to be involved in the ministry of the Sunday School class. Get others involved in prayer, visitation, and leadership. In Phil. 1:27 the apostle Paul encourages us to stand together in one spirit. We're to live with a spirit of cooperation. We're to stand side-by-side as soldiers. We're to stand united as gladiators striving against a common enemy for a common cause. As we work together, God works in powerful ways.

Prayer: *Lord, I'm thankful for your wonderful gift of friends and partners in ministry. I pray for all those who serve with me. I pray that you would give us a unity of heart, purpose, and desire to see you honored and exalted. In your Son's name I pray. Amen.*

THE PEOPLE IN JUDAH SAID, "THE STRENGTH OF THE
LABORERS IS GIVING OUT, AND THERE IS SO MUCH
RUBBLE THAT WE CANNOT REBUILD THE WALL."
—Neh. 4:10

ACCOMPLISHING ANY LARGE TASK IS TIRING.
THERE ARE ALWAYS PRESSURES THAT FOSTER
DISCOURAGEMENT—THE TASK SEEMS IMPOSSIBLE,
IT CAN NEVER BE FINISHED, OR TOO MANY FACTORS
ARE WORKING AGAINST US. THE ONLY CURE
FOR FATIGUE AND DISCOURAGEMENT IS
FOCUSING ON GOD'S PURPOSES.
—*Life Application Bible* notes

DOWN BUT NOT OUT

*We do not want you to be uninformed, brothers, about the hardships
we suffered in the province of Asia. We were under great pressure,
far beyond our ability to endure, so that we despaired even of life.*
—2 Cor. 1:8

John Henry Jowett was called in his day the greatest
preacher in the English-speaking world. He was the pastor
of the most influential churches, preached to huge congrega-
tions, and wrote books that were best sellers. He wrote:

You seem to imagine that I have no ups and downs, but
just a level and lofty stretch of spiritual attainment with
unbroken joy and serenity. By no means! I am often perfectly wretched and everything appears most murky.

Charles Haddon Spurgeon wrote:

I am the subject of depressions of spirit so fearful that I
hope none of you ever get to such extremes of wretched-
ness as I go to.

Spurgeon spoke these words in a sermon. His marvelous ministry in London made him one of the greatest preachers England ever produced.

Discouragement is no respecter of persons. In fact, it seems to attack the successful far more than the unsuccessful. The higher we climb, the farther down we can fall. We should not be surprised when we read that the great apostle Paul was "under great pressure" and "despaired even of life." As great as he was in character and ministry, he was human, just like the rest of us.

In Paul's writing in 2 Cor. 1:1-11 one of the key words is "comfort." The Greek word means "to strengthen" or "to be called to one's side to help." The verb is used 18 times in this letter, the noun 11 times. In spite of all the trials he experienced, Paul was able by the grace of God to write a letter saturated with comfort and encouragement.

Sometimes as a Sunday School teacher you may find yourself discouraged because of disappointing attendance or difficult circumstances. At those times it's easy to look at ourselves or to focus on the problems around us. What was Paul's secret of victory when he was experiencing pressures and trials? It was his focus on God. When you find yourself discouraged and ready to quit, get your attention off yourself and focus on God. We can, as Paul tells us, find encouragement in God.

Prayer: *Lord, in times of discouragement, help me stay focused on you. Give me the strength to finish the tasks that seem impossible.*

I WILL GIVE YOU SHEPHERDS AFTER MY OWN HEART,
WHO WILL LEAD YOU WITH KNOWLEDGE AND
UNDERSTANDING.
—Jer. 3:15

FOLLOW GOD, AND SEEK HIS GUIDANCE AND
DIRECTION SO YOU CAN LEAD YOUR STUDENTS
IN THE WAY THEY SHOULD GO.
—David Graves

FEED MY LAMBS

When they had finished eating, Jesus said to Simon Peter,
"Simon son of John, do you truly love me more than these?" "Yes, Lord,"
he said, "you know that I love you." Jesus said, "Feed my lambs."
—John 21:15

Jesus reminds us of the frailty of our children and their spiritual lives. Andrew Murray was once leaving a sheep farm after visiting with the owner and noticed threatening clouds. He hurried back, crying out to his son, "Take care of the lambs! There's a storm coming!"

Just before our Lord Jesus ascended to heaven, one of His last commands was to care for the lambs. Sheep are weak and helpless animals. How much more helpless is the little lamb! It cannot care for itself.

Jesus wants us to realize how dependent the child is on the care of those to whom he or she is entrusted. As infants, children are totally dependent on adults for everything. As youngsters, children are still dependent. A child cannot choose the persons who influence him or her, the language he or she hears, or the habits he or she observes. The child does not yet know how to choose between good and evil. He or she knows nothing of the importance of little words or deeds, of forming habits, of sowing good or bad seed, or of yielding to the world or God. All depends upon the child's surroundings.

What a solemn responsibility we have to children as a church and as Sunday School teachers to direct and nourish them carefully, to lead them in the green pastures, and to guide and provide for their spiritual wellbeing.

Prayer: *"The* LORD *is my Shepherd; I shall not want"* (Ps. 23:1, KJV). *Lord, I thank you for your spiritual nourishment and refreshment. As you feed me, help me feed your people from the overflow of your abundant provision to me. In Jesus' name I pray. Amen.*

IF YOU FORGIVE MEN WHEN THEY SIN AGAINST YOU,
YOUR HEAVENLY FATHER WILL ALSO FORGIVE YOU. BUT
IF YOU DO NOT FORGIVE MEN THEIR SINS, YOUR
FATHER WILL NOT FORGIVE YOUR SINS.
—Matt. 6:14-15

IT IS EASY TO ASK GOD FOR FORGIVENESS,
BUT DIFFICULT TO GRANT IT TO OTHERS. WHENEVER
WE ASK GOD TO FORGIVE US FOR SIN, WE SHOULD
ASK OURSELVES, "HAVE I FORGIVEN THE
PEOPLE WHO HAVE WRONGED ME?"
—*Life Application Bible* notes

FORGIVENESS

*If you forgive anyone, I also forgive him. And what I have forgiven—if there
was anything to forgive—I have forgiven in the sight of Christ for your sake.*
—2 Cor. 2:10

How do we respond when we're insulted and hurt? Paul had
personally been insulted by the individual in question; yet
notice how freely he extends forgiveness in 2 Cor. 2:10.

There are no hard feelings expressed, no recriminations,
no "well, I'll-forgive-but-I-can't-forget" attitude. You often hear
that, don't you? That reveals a lack of understanding of what
forgiveness is. Forgiveness is basically a promise you make to
the individual who has offended you and repented, in which
you're saying to him or her, "I will not let my attitude toward
you be governed any longer by this offense—it has been put
aside. My treatment of you from here on will be as though this
has never happened."

It's a promise not to bring it up again. In marriage, many
problems go on for years and years because we dig up the
past. This is an indication that it has never been forgiven.
Some mates don't get hysterical—they get *historical*!

Not only must we forgive, but we're also to forget. The first way to forget is to stop talking about it to other people. We need to drop the matter, leave it in the past, and never bring it up again. The second way to forget is that when your memory goes back to it (as it may occasionally), don't allow it to seize hold of your heart and make you angry all over again. The minute it comes to your mind, put it aside as something that belongs to the past—you're not going to dwell on it.

That's forgiveness, and Paul was so ready to forgive. He could forgive because he himself had been forgiven. He wrote, "Be kind and compassionate to one another, forgiving each other, just as in Christ God forgave you" (Eph. 4:32).

There will be times when people hurt your feelings, talk about you in a negative way, or even leave your class. Be willing to forgive them, and move forward with God.

Prayer: *Lord, I praise you for the forgiveness of all my sins. Help me forgive those who have sinned or wronged me. I choose to forgive as you have forgiven so I can move forward in my relationship with you. In Christ's name I pray. Amen.*

NOW GET UP AND STAND ON YOUR FEET. I HAVE
APPEARED TO YOU TO APPOINT YOU AS A SERVANT
AND AS A WITNESS OF WHAT YOU HAVE SEEN
OF ME AND WHAT I WILL SHOW YOU.
—Acts 26:16

PAUL WAS MADE A MINISTER BY DIVINE AUTHORITY:
THE SAME JESUS WHO APPEARED TO HIM IN THAT
GLORIOUS LIGHT ORDERED HIM TO PREACH
THE GOSPEL TO THE GENTILES. A WORLD THAT
SITS IN DARKNESS MUST BE ENLIGHTENED;
THOSE MUST BE BROUGHT TO KNOW THE
THINGS THAT BELONG TO THEIR EVERLASTING
PEACE, WHO ARE YET IGNORANT OF THEM.
—Matthew Henry

GOD SPEAKS

*The LORD came and stood there, calling as at the other times, "Samuel!
Samuel!" Then Samuel said, "Speak, for your servant is listening."*
—1 Sam. 3:10

Throughout the pages of the Bible we find a God who loves us and wants the very best for each of us—and will go to great lengths to reach us.

Bob was raised in a Christian home. By the time he was 16, he had given up trying to please God. As a typical adolescent, he figured he was always offending God with one sin or another. He decided to put religion behind him. One day while working in Wyandotte, Michigan, he decided to eat lunch at the Big Boy restaurant there. He sat at the counter, and it seemed as if no one knew he was in the restaurant. As Bob was eating his lunch, he felt a tap on his shoulder. He turned around to see a scholarly looking man. The stranger looked at Bob and said, "I want to see you in church."

Bob was dumbfounded and even embarrassed. *Why me?* he thought. He wasn't attending church at the time and admitted he was behaving in less-than-holy ways. At first he thought the man was soliciting for his own church, so Bob informed the stranger that he didn't live in Wyandotte. "I didn't say *which* church," the man replied. "I said I want to see you in church."

Bob swiveled away for just few seconds to mull over the strange comment. When he turned back, the man was gone. He looked all over the restaurant but didn't see the stranger anywhere. When he got home he told his wife what had happened. They decided that if God would go to all this trouble to get them into church, then they ought to give it some thought. Not long afterward, Bob and his wife joined a church.

God cares about all people. He does speak. Sometimes He speaks through miraculous intervention, at other times through a preacher, a teacher, a song, an event. Thank God that we're serving a God who loves, cares, and speaks. Thank God for speaking through you and your teaching.

Prayer: *Lord, I've heard you speak in many different ways. Thank you that you're a God who speaks to your children. May you continue to give me insight and wisdom as I teach the Bible. May those in the class hear you speak through my teaching. In Jesus' name I pray. Amen.*

BUT BY THE GRACE OF GOD I AM WHAT I AM, AND
HIS GRACE TO ME WAS NOT WITHOUT EFFECT. NO, I
WORKED HARDER THAN ALL OF THEM—YET NOT I,
BUT THE GRACE OF GOD THAT WAS WITH ME.
—1 Cor. 15:10

TRUE HUMILITY IS NOT CONVINCING YOURSELF THAT
YOU ARE WORTHLESS, BUT RECOGNIZING GOD'S WORK
IN YOU. IT IS HAVING GOD'S PERSPECTIVE ON WHO
YOU ARE AND ACKNOWLEDGING HIS GRACE IN
DEVELOPING YOUR ABILITIES.
—*Life Application Bible* notes

GRACE

*To the church of the Thessalonians in God the Father and the
Lord Jesus Christ: Grace and peace to you.*
—1 Thess. 1:1

*I*f I had to select one word to describe the nature of God, it
would be "grace." The word flashes like a diamond held up
to the light. It means giving, forgiving, unchanging, unmoti-
vated, and unconditional love. God relates to us with accept-
ing and affirming love.

The Cross is the sublime expression of unqualified love.
Before we were ready, deserving, and worthy, Christ died for
us.

The apostle Paul never forgot that grace. It was the ethos of
his thinking, the ambience of his living, and the motivation of
his ministry. He constantly remembered the unlimited grace
he experienced on the Damascus road. He was transformed
from being a persecutor of the faith to becoming a most vigilant preacher. Paul went from being a self-righteous man to a
Christ-reconciled new creation. He went from hostility toward
life to an inexhaustible hope. For Paul, grace meant to live in

Christ and allow Christ to live in him. He was filled with the indwelling Christ himself. Paul became a powerful man, because Christ literally took up residence in him.

The greatest need in our Sunday School classes is for those of us who have believed in Christ to be filled with Him. We need to be filled with His presence, His power, and His passion. An authentic person is one who is being transformed into His image. The more we experience His amazing grace, the more we can yield our minds and hearts to be His post-Resurrection home. We begin to view our problems as merely a prelude to fresh grace. Our problems bring us to the end of ourselves and to the place of openness in which He can fill us with himself.

As a Sunday School teacher, surrender your brain to thinking His thoughts, your emotions to be channels of His warmth and love. Paul learned this repeatedly. The Lord's Word to him was "My grace is sufficient for you, for my power is made perfect in weakness" (2 Cor. 12:9).

The exciting news for all Sunday School teachers is that Christ's grace is indeed sufficient for all our problems, fears, failures, trials, weaknesses, challenges, and tasks.

Prayer: *Lord, I surrender myself to your grace today. I know that your grace is sufficient for all my problems, fears, failures, trials, weaknesses, challenges, and tasks. May you work in and through me.*

To him who is able to keep you from falling
and to present you before his glorious presence
without fault and with great joy—to the only
God our Savior be glory, majesty, power and
authority, through Jesus Christ our Lord,
before all ages, now and forevermore! Amen.
—Jude 24-25

Let us more often look up to Him who is able
to keep us from falling, to improve as well as
maintain the work He has wrought in us, till
we shall be presented blameless before the
presence of His glory. Then shall our hearts
know a joy beyond what earth can afford;
then shall God also rejoice over us, and the
joy of our compassionate Savior be completed.
—Matthew Henry

GUARDING OUR DEPOSIT

Guard the good deposit that was entrusted to you—
guard it with the help of the Holy Spirit who lives in us.
—2 Tim. 1:14

How do we guard our deposit? When the multimillionaire Andrew Carnegie was building a new home, he instructed the architect to place the following inscription over the living room fireplace: "This hearth is our family altar. Its warmth reminds us of Christ's presence in our home." After the house and fireplace were completed, the architect went to Carnegie and said, "You'll have to choose another motto—that one is too long to fit over the fireplace!"

"No!" said the millionaire. "I want those words. If you must, then tear down the fireplace and build a bigger one."

The architect informed him, "Sir, you cannot build a bigger fireplace without building a bigger room!"

"All right" was the reply. "Tear out the walls and build a bigger room!"

The architect then said, "But a bigger room will throw the entire house out of proportion!"

"Then tear the entire house down and start over," the millionaire said, "for we must have that motto as a constant reminder that Christ is in our home!"

We could say that Andrew Carnegie built his home around the conviction that Jesus Christ was central in his family. Are you building your home around that same conviction? Does your daily life reflect the truth that you really believe Christ is present in your home? Do you show your family that Christ is central to your home by praying with them? Or is the prayer in Sunday morning worship service the only time your family prays together? Are you demonstrating to your family the importance of Bible reading by having daily devotions, or is Sunday morning the only time you have contact with the Word? Are your actions, your speech, and your love proclaiming the presence of Christ in your home, or do they demonstrate that you really left the Lord back at the church?

Are you building your Sunday School class around the conviction that Jesus Christ is central to your class? There are other things you can build your class around: teaching, fellowship, social activities, sharing of personal issues. None of these are bad—just make sure Jesus Christ is central if you want to build and maintain a strong Sunday School class.

Prayer: *Lord, I pray that you will be the center of my life. I pray that you will be the center of my class. May you always be exalted, lifted up, and honored in all I do. In your Son's name I pray. Amen.*

NONE OF US LIVES TO HIMSELF ALONE AND
NONE OF US DIES TO HIMSELF ALONE.

—Rom. 14:7

MY LIFE OF SERVICE TO GOD IS THE WAY
I SAY "THANK YOU" TO HIM FOR HIS
INEXPRESSIBLY WONDERFUL SALVATION.

—Oswald Chambers

HERE IS A BOY

*Here is a boy with five small barley loaves and two small fish,
but how far will they go among so many?*
—John 6:9

When Robert Moffat returned to Scotland after years of Christian service in Africa, his main purpose was to recruit workers. Speaking at one church on a cold winter night, he was discouraged to find only a small group of women as his congregation. The whole design of his message that night had been aimed toward men. It was completely the wrong message for this particular group. Not a man was in the house.

However, in the loft, pumping the organ bellows, was a small boy who listened intently to the earnest missionary and was deeply challenged. He promised God that he would follow in this great man's steps. When this boy grew up, he went to Africa and became one of the world's most famous missionaries. His name? David Livingstone.

Many fine pastors have gone to their graves without seeing much fruit from their ministry. But somewhere a small boy or girl or young person or adult was hearing the voice of God speak through the pastor, and it had a dramatic effect on his or her life.

There are many dedicated Sunday School teachers who have gone home with heavy hearts because their class did not respond as they had hoped. But remember: seeds are being sown in the classroom, and some day will come a harvest.

In John 6 we find the story of the feeding of the multitude. Great crowds were pressing in to be taught by Jesus. How were they to be fed? There was not enough money in the treasury to feed a gathering that large, and a McDonald's was not nearby.

During the period in which this story took place, children were not counted in the attendance. It's very possible that no one else among the disciples noticed this young boy among the vast throng. But Andrew did, and he told Jesus, "Here is a boy with five barley loaves and two small fish." The young boy's lunch and willingness to give became the foundation for the miracle and nourishment of a multitude of people.

Engraved on some pulpits in our land are the words from John 12:21, "Sir, we would see Jesus" (KJV). I would contend it would be equally as meaningful if every teacher were reminded before going into the classroom, "Here is a boy . . ."

Prayer: *Lord, you performed a miracle because of the faithfulness and surrender of a little boy. May you take the little I have and work spiritual miracles in the lives of those in my class. I surrender myself to you. In Jesus' name I pray. Amen.*

WHO IS WISE AND UNDERSTANDING AMONG YOU?
LET HIM SHOW IT BY HIS GOOD LIFE, BY DEEDS DONE
IN THE HUMILITY THAT COMES FROM WISDOM.
—James 3:13

AS TEACHERS OF GOD'S WORD, LET US LIVE A LIFE OF
SUCH BEAUTIFUL GRACIOUSNESS THAT WE WILL PROVE
TO ALL THAT GENTLENESS IS ENTHRONED AS THE
CONTROLLING POWER WITHIN OUR HEARTS.
—William Barclay

REMAINING CONSISTENT
IN CHANGING TIMES

*Whatever happens, conduct yourselves in a manner worthy of the gospel of
Christ. Then, whether I come and see you or only hear about you in my
absence, I will know that you stand firm in one spirit, contending as one man
for the faith of the gospel without being frightened in any way by those who
oppose you. This is a sign to them that they will be destroyed, but that you
will be saved—and that by God. For it has been granted to you on behalf
of Christ not only to believe on him, but also to suffer for him.*
—Phil. 1:27-29

The leaning Tower of Pisa is the tower of the Cathedral of
Pisa in Italy. It is shaped like a cylinder and is made of
white marble. In all, it has eight arcades, one over the other. A
spiral staircase leads to the top. Shortly after the completion of
the structure, it was noticed that the tower was beginning to
lean, because the ground below it was the beginning to sink.
Through the centuries the tower has continued and increased
its leaning. Today it is leaning almost 14 feet.

Some Christians are like this famous tower. They go to
church and associate with Christians, yet you can't tell they're
Christians by the fruit of their lives, actions, and behavior.
Some Christians are leaning toward the world instead of God.

They're not willing to be obedient to what God wants them to do. The apostle Paul was a man who was willing to pay the price to be obedient to Christ. He was consistent in his life and character regardless of the changes in his life. In Phil. 1:27-29 he encourages us to be consistent in the midst of changing times.

What does it mean to let our manner of life be worthy of the gospel? Philippi was a proud Roman state. Its people acted like Romans, talked like Romans, and dressed like Romans. The Philippians were proud to be Roman and took advantage of the privilege of being Roman.

The same is true for our heavenly citizenship. We're to fulfill our duties and responsibilities as Christians and to be consistent in our behavior. If we profess to believe in God, we should act worthy of the profession. Profess it and then live like it. Your students learn from listening to your teaching, but they also learn from observing your life. May you be godly and consistent in your conduct!

Prayer: *Lord, help me not only to talk the talk but also to walk the walk. I desire to be like you. Help me to be consistent in my behavior. Help me to live a life worthy of being called one of your children. In Christ's name I pray. Amen.*

STAND FIRM. LET NOTHING MOVE YOU.
ALWAYS GIVE YOURSELVES FULLY TO THE WORK
OF THE LORD, BECAUSE YOU KNOW THAT
YOUR LABOR IN THE LORD IS NOT IN VAIN.
—1 Cor. 15:58

AS A TEACHER, DON'T LET DISCOURAGEMENT OR
DISAPPOINTMENT OVER AN APPARENT LACK OF RESULTS
KEEP YOU FROM WORKING FOR GOD. DO THE GOOD
THAT YOU HAVE OPPORTUNITY TO DO, KNOWING
THAT YOUR WORK WILL HAVE ETERNAL RESULTS.

WORDS

No matter how many promises God has made, they are "Yes" in Christ.
And so through him the "Amen" is spoken by us to the glory of God.
—2 Cor. 1:20

Words are odd things. You can use them to reveal your thoughts or to conceal them. Few of us can honestly say we mean every word we say. We may say something because it appears to be the right thing to say. We may say something for the sake of being agreeable. We may say it for the sake of avoiding trouble.

God is not like that—He is faithful to His Word. When God says yes, it is an eternal yes. He will never take it back. When God says no, He means no.

He never says yes when He means no. Paul tells us God's promises are always positive promises. Have you noticed that in the Scriptures? In Christ it is always yes. God's promises are not for cursing but for blessing. They are not for condemnation— they are for salvation. Jesus did not come to take life from us; rather, He came to revive us and give us life more abundantly (John 10:10). God does not come to reject but to restore.

To bestow on them a crown of beauty instead of ashes, the oil of gladness instead of mourning, and a garment of praise instead of a spirit of despair. They will be called oaks of righteousness, a planting of the LORD for the display of his splendor *(Isa. 61:3)*.

According to Paul, all this is available to us in Christ. We can actually begin to experience it when we cling to His Word and say amen to God's promise. When you read one of His hundreds of promises and you say, "That's for me, Lord. I want that," you begin to obey the qualification or the commitment the promise demands. Then the promise begins to be real in your life.

As a teacher of the Word of God, make sure you personally claim His promises for your own life. The way to find God's blessing is to respond to His promise by claiming it for yourself and saying, "Lord, that promise is mine. Amen—I believe."

Prayer: *Lord, I claim your promises. I desire to experience your blessing in my life. I receive the abundant life you have promised to those who seek you. In your Son's name I pray. Amen.*

I CAN DO EVERYTHING THROUGH HIM
WHO GIVES ME STRENGTH.
—Phil. 4:13

FOCUS ON THE POSITIVE!

HOPE

"I know the plans I have for you," declares the LORD, "plans to prosper
you and not to harm you, plans to give you hope and a future."
—Jer. 29:11

The world is a hopeless place, but not without hope.
Read the headlines or watch the evening news. You'll
see a depressing picture, a world out of control: soldiers dying
in the desert, children abandoned by their parents, a world-
wide AIDS epidemic. The news is never good.

Except in Sunday School.

Here is where we set the record straight. God is on his
throne. Jesus Christ is alive. There is a reason to be optimistic
about the future. God knows something that we don't. He not
only knows the end of the story—He wrote it. And nothing
between now and then will happen without His knowledge or
approval.

Always teach the good news. Prove to your students that
with Christ the future is always brighter than the past. Be positive. Teach positively. The Bible has more promises than
problems. "God has a plan." And that plan is for your good—
and the good of your students.

Your students arrive for Sunday School carrying the weight
of the world on their shoulders. They don't have to leave that
way. You can lighten their loads. You can give them hope. You
can assure them that their Creator has everything under control. But you can't do that without believing it yourself. Your
lesson of hope doesn't come from your head—it comes from

your heart and is planted there by your knowledge of the Bible and its last pages.

Prayer: *Father, let the hope of your Word be evidenced on my face and in my words. But first let me know your hope in my heart. Teach me to cast my care on you and discover from my study how much you care for me. In Jesus' name I pray. Amen.*

HOW GREAT IS THE LOVE THE FATHER HAS
LAVISHED ON US, THAT WE SHOULD BE CALLED
CHILDREN OF GOD! AND THAT IS WHAT WE ARE!
THE REASON THE WORLD DOES NOT KNOW US
IS THAT IT DID NOT KNOW HIM.

—1 John 3:1

LOVE WITH THE LOVE OF GOD.

LOVE

If I speak in the tongues of men and of angels, but have not love,
I am only a resounding gong or a clanging cymbal.
—1 Cor. 13:1

You have only one job—to love your students.

As a Sunday School teacher, you have many responsibilities. You must be knowledgeable of Scripture. You must possess classroom skill. You must be part prayer warrior, part coach, part social secretary.

But none of these roles is your real job. Your ultimate responsibility is to give students the one thing they need more than programs, knowledge, or skill. Your real job is to love your students unconditionally. You must make the Cross personal; you must make sure your students understand that the arms stretched wide reach all the way around them.

Drugs, peer pressure, school, family problems, physical adversity—students bring a world of hurt into the classroom with them. They're hurting; some are broken. And you have what they need. Love is the best medicine, and there's plenty to go around. Open your heart. Open your arms. Love your students.

George W. Bush said, "Grief, tragedy, and hatred are only for a time. Goodness, remembrance, and love have no end." Love your students. You're planting seeds that will bloom in eternity.

Prayer: *Lord, you loved me unconditionally. The Cross proves it, and I've found it in you. Help me to personally rest in your love. And let your love flow through me to my students—in word, in deed, in my attitude, and in my understanding. In Christ's name I pray. Amen.*

IT WAS HE WHO GAVE SOME TO BE APOSTLES,
SOME TO BE PROPHETS, SOME TO BE EVANGELISTS,
AND SOME TO BE PASTORS AND TEACHERS,
TO PREPARE GOD'S PEOPLE FOR WORKS OF SERVICE,
SO THAT THE BODY OF CHRIST MAY BE BUILT UP.
—Eph. 4:11-12

TEACHING IS A DIVINE CALLING.

AMBITION

I will give you every place where you set your foot,
as I promised Moses.
—Josh. 1:3

*D*on't be a teacher unless you want to change the world.
It's in there, deep within your heart. It's that nagging feeling that there's a "big thing" you should be doing with your life. It's your ambition to do something great in the world—something great for God.

And it's a good thing. God gave it to you when He called you, saved you, and set you apart to work for His kingdom. Your appointment wasn't an accident. You may have doubts about your ability. But remember—God put that holy ambition within you. The fire that engulfs your soul when you think about your lesson or your class comes from above.

And He will see that your ambition is fulfilled. Your job is to be faithful. You're to do the work that He has assigned to you. Every week plant the seed. Water it. Tend the field. And God will give the increase. You may not see it now. It may show up at your door or in a letter. Your work will not be in vain. It's a promise:

As the rain and the snow come down from heaven, and do not return to it without watering the earth and making it bud and flourish, so that it yields seed for the sower and bread for the eater, so is my word that goes out from my mouth: It will not return to me empty, but will accomplish what I desire and achieve the purpose for which I sent it (Isa. 55:10-11).

Some people get up in the morning and have nothing to do but make money, win applause, or rule nations. You have better things to do—you teach Sunday School class.

Prayer: *Lord, thank you for your great grace that's available to accomplish my big job. In Jesus' name I pray. Amen.*

DEAR FRIENDS, NOW WE ARE CHILDREN OF GOD,
AND WHAT WE WILL BE HAS NOT YET BEEN MADE
KNOWN. BUT WE KNOW THAT WHEN HE APPEARS,
WE SHALL BE LIKE HIM, FOR WE SHALL SEE HIM
AS HE IS. EVERYONE WHO HAS THIS HOPE
IN HIM PURIFIES HIMSELF, JUST AS HE IS PURE.

—1 John 3:2-3

PREPARE STUDENTS FOR GOD'S TOMORROWS.

ETERNITY

*He has made everything beautiful in its time. He has also
set eternity in the hearts of men; yet they cannot fathom
what God has done from beginning to end.*
—Eccles. 3:11

A Sunday School teacher's work is never done—it goes on forever.

Some weekends it seems it will never end. It starts early, before you ever arrive at church. Your own kids are unruly. The car won't start. You forget your Bible at the house.

At church it gets no better. Everyone seems to arrive late and in a poor mood. You read the scripture, and people yawn. You tell a funny story, and there isn't as much as a chuckle. You ask for volunteers; there are none.

Will it ever end?

Yes, the day will end. And yes, your time of service as a Sunday School teacher will end. There will come a day when there are no lessons to prepare, no skits to rehearse, no classes to teach, and no students to mentor.

It will all be over.

But in another sense, your work as a Sunday School teacher will never truly end. The seeds that you have planted will continue to grow. The lives that you have touched will in turn touch others. The work that you have done will go on—well, forever.

It's not just about one weekend, one class session, one lesson. It's about placing the concept of eternity in the hearts and minds of your students. They must know that life never ends, that they will spend eternity either in the presence of God or away from His presence. That message begins with you. With your heart fixed on eternity—watch for eternal results.

Prayer: *Father, thank you for reminding me that what I do now will last forever. Give me the wisdom to remind my students that the decisions they make now will make an eternal difference. In Christ's name I pray. Amen.*

I PLANTED THE SEED, APOLLOS WATERED IT,
BUT GOD MADE IT GROW.
—1 Cor. 3:6

WE ARE BLESSED TO BLESS!

BLESSING

Blessed are those who hunger and thirst for righteousness,
for they will be filled.
—Matt. 5:6

*Y*ou are doing a good thing with your life.

Never doubt that your work is worthwhile. It may be true that it is underappreciated. Students fail to pay attention. Parents complain about schedules. Elderly folks have too many answers. Young people are distracted. Volunteers are uncooperative.

But your life is a blessing just the same.

You teach the Word to those who may not otherwise hear it. You are a blessing.

You show love to those who are desperate for loving attention. You are a blessing.

You model patience and compassion and perseverance to waiting minds. You are a blessing.

You give of yourself freely, gladly, fully. You are a blessing.

Your deepest desire is to be like Jesus. You want to know Him, to understand Him, to become like Him.

And when you love your students, when you teach the truth, when you give generously to others, you *are* like Him.

Blessed are you, Sunday Sschool teacher. For that which you desire has been made real. Christ has poured His very life into your willing service. On any given weekend, you are the hands and feet and tongue of the Savior. His Holy Spirit leads you in what seems to be mundane but what is actually life-changing.

You are a blessing because you are blessed. Your worth is in the hands and heart of the One who made you worthy.

Prayer: *Jesus, thank you for blessing me and for making me a blessing. I may not have a lot of experience, but I have a great teacher: One who fed the 5,000 precious people on a hillside both with bread and with the Bread of Life. I'm blessed by your presence whenever I represent you to my class. In your name I pray. Amen.*

CHRIST DID NOT SEND ME TO BAPTIZE,
BUT TO PREACH THE GOSPEL—NOT WITH WORDS
OF HUMAN WISDOM, LEST THE CROSS OF
CHRIST BE EMPTIED OF ITS POWER.
—1 Cor. 1:17

TEACH TO INFLUENCE LIVES.

FRUIT

I am the vine; you are the branches. If a man remains in me and I in him,
he will bear much fruit; apart from me you can do nothing.
—John 15:5

You can't do this alone.

Teaching the Bible is too big a job for you. You're not smart enough. You're not skilled enough. You're not righteous enough. You don't have what it takes to be a mentor, teacher, coach, and guide.

The good news is that you don't have to be. Jesus gave you a promise: "You will receive power when the Holy Spirit comes on you; and you will be my witnesses in Jerusalem, and in all Judea and Samaria, and to the ends of the earth" (Acts 1:8). Did you catch the sequence? "You will . . ." "when . . ."

No one ever said that you had to be all-wise, all-caring, all-good in order to be a teacher. In fact, you can't be. But with the power of the Holy Spirit, you *can* teach. The Spirit has called you for this work, and the Spirit will equip you to succeed in it.

Your task? Abide in Christ.

For when you know Him better, love Him more fully, devote yourself to Him more completely, then you will bear much fruit—fruit that will last. Teaching is more than delivering a lesson. It is personally claiming the resources of God for a moment in time—class time. It's an exciting opportunity. It's like plugging an extension cord into an outlet and expecting it to light a lamp or start an appliance feet or yards away.

That's teaching—plugging into the Holy Spirit's power source and bringing spiritual light or energy to those who sit feet or yards away.

Prayer: *Holy Spirit, make me a channel of your power and light. Use me to bring truth to a needy heart. Allow me to be an extension of the Christ for the teaching assignment you have called me to—and equipped me for. In Jesus' name I pray. Amen.*

THIS IS MY PRAYER: THAT YOUR LOVE MAY ABOUND
MORE AND MORE IN KNOWLEDGE AND DEPTH OF
INSIGHT, SO THAT YOU MAY BE ABLE TO DISCERN
WHAT IS BEST AND MAY BE PURE AND BLAMELESS UNTIL
THE DAY OF CHRIST, FILLED WITH THE FRUIT OF
RIGHTEOUSNESS THAT COMES THROUGH JESUS
CHRIST—TO THE GLORY AND PRAISE OF GOD.
—Phil. 1:9-11

THE WALK MUST MATCH THE TALK.

AUTHENTICITY

*Woe to you, teachers of the law and Pharisees, you hypocrites! You give a
tenth of your spices—mint, dill and cummin. But you have neglected the
more important matters of the law—justice, mercy and faithfulness.
You should have practiced the latter, without neglecting the former.*
—Matt. 23:23

*I*f you are not real, you are nothing.

Teachers of the Bible are prone to a particular pitfall. It
has been this way since Bible times. We know the Scriptures
well. We understand the rules. We know—better than anyone
else—what righteousness looks like.

That means we can fake it if we choose.

Resist the temptation to be something that you're not. Be
transparent. Be authentic. Be real.

When you don't know the answer, say so. When you've
failed, admit it. When you need to apologize, do so promptly.
You're only human—and everyone knows it. There's no need
to pretend otherwise.

Where does that kind of authenticity come from? First, it
comes from being honest with God. As the psalmist David
said, "Search me, O God, and know my heart; test me and
know my anxious thoughts" (Ps. 139:23). A heart open to the
scanning of the Holy Spirit is a heart that's willing to be used

to carry a spiritual burden for others. God can use a tiny vessel—but He can't use a dirty vessel.

Be honest with your students. One of the greatest gifts you can give your students is to model for them what it means to be a sincere follower of Jesus Christ.

Prayer: *Father, I open my heart to you. Search my every affection, my every motive, and my every attitude. I want to be an authentic servant of yours. In Jesus' name I pray. Amen.*

WISDOM

*If any of you lacks wisdom, he should ask God, who gives generously
to all without finding fault, and it will be given to him.*
—James 1:5

Seek God.

There are lots of good things that you can do to prepare yourself to teach. You can study the Scriptures, and you should. You need to be a skilled craftsman, accurately handling the Word of God.

You can develop your craft, and you will. You will gain skill at speaking in public, conducting discussions, training minds. You will help yourself to become a better teacher.

But there's one thing that's more important than the rest: you must seek God.

Seek His wisdom for providing insight to eager young Christians. Some won't know the difference between justification and sanctification—or care about either. But God can give you wisdom to enlighten them, lesson by lesson, week by week.

Seek His compassion for dealing with difficult life situations. A great teacher not only has a mind for study but also has a shoulder for sympathy. For that hour—or less—you are the shepherd, the encourager. You'll learn to look at a suffering soul with the face of understanding.

Seek His heart for coping with trying circumstances in the classroom. Depending on the age-group, you'll either dodge folded Sunday School leaflets or sidestep distracting questions. God will give you wisdom for both.

Seek His holiness to make you a man or woman of God, a representation of His Son, Jesus Christ. You can't burn with enthusiasm until you've been close to the fire. Go for the genuine.

Seek the mind of God, and you'll find it in His Word.

Prayer: *Lord, help me to drink deeply from the wells of your wisdom. I praise you for the help you will give to me. In the name of your wonderful Son, Jesus, I pray. Amen.*

WHERE THERE IS NO REVELATION,
THE PEOPLE CAST OFF RESTRAINT;
BUT BLESSED IS HE WHO KEEPS THE LAW.
—Prov. 29:18

YOU HAVE TO BELIEVE IT TO SEE IT.

VISION

The word of the LORD came to me: "What do you see, Jeremiah?" "I see the branch of an almond tree," I replied. The LORD said to me, "You have seen correctly, for I am watching to see that my word is fulfilled."
—Jer. 1:11-12

Look for the future, and it will be revealed by God.
When God calls a prophet, He gives that prophet a vision of the future. That need not be an apocalyptic vision of doom and destruction. God simply reveals to His messenger a picture of the world the way it ought to be—the way it *will* be if God's Word is obeyed.

God has placed that vision before your eyes. Do you see it? Do you see young people growing in their faith, becoming the leaders of tomorrow's Church?

Do you see troubled souls rescued from a life of addiction and violence?

Do you see God's church growing in number, growing in faith, growing in strength?

Do you see the world different from what it is today?

That's a vision of what will be if you and I are faithful in our task as teachers. New converts will be won to the faith. Young believers will be strengthened in the Lord. God's Church will multiply its impact upon the world. Revival will blossom in the desert of these times.

Can you see it?

Prayer: *Jesus, help me look at my class with your eyes. Help me see beyond the immediate into the future. Open my heart to the heavenly possibilities represented in my class. In Your powerful name I pray. Amen.*

MY HEART IS SET ON KEEPING YOUR
DECREES TO THE VERY END.
—Ps. 119:112

THE BIBLE MUST HAVE NO RIVAL.

IMAGINATION

No eye has seen, no ear has heard, no mind has conceived
what God has prepared for those who love him.
—1 Cor. 2:9

*I*t's a terrible thing to bore people with the Word of God.

The Bible contains the most exciting words ever written. Within its pages are things one can barely believe. In it the sun stands still. Waters are parted. Mountains are removed. Giants are slain.

It contains adventures and quests and battles of epic proportions. There are within this book the sagas of great heroes and cowardly villains. City walls collapse at the sound of trumpets. Kingdoms fall because of one man's sin. One man stands against an entire army. One woman overturns an entire kingdom. Little children lead adults into faith. Older folks serve as spiritual role models.

This book contains poems and love songs and rousing tales far more clever than Dante's or Shakespeare's. The Bible is the record of real-life intrigue, of politics, plotting, and betrayal.

This book contains words of hope, words of forgiveness, words that all people crave and seldom find. It's a book without comparison and surely a book with imagination. "There's gold" in these hills of truths. But it must be mined—mined by letting its sacred stories fill your imagination. Put yourself on its battlefields. Sit by the still waters of its beauty. Stand on the rock of its promises. The imagination you foster in the lives of others will be born in times of studying and meditating on each of the sacred scenes.

Students will enter your classroom bored, and with good reason. Introduce them to the Word of God. They'll never be bored again.

Prayer: *Father, give me the ability to bring your truth to life in my study and in my teaching. In Jesus' name I pray. Amen.*

BROTHERS, MY HEART'S DESIRE AND PRAYER TO GOD
FOR THE ISRAELITES IS THAT THEY MAY BE SAVED.
—Rom. 10:1

TEACH WITH A BURNING HEART.

ENTHUSIASM

His disciples remembered that it is written:
"Zeal for your house will consume me."
—John 2:17

Teaching isn't a job—it's a passion.

If you can be happy doing something on Sunday morning besides teaching Sunday School, do it. Teaching is for those of us who can't.

Teaching is a calling, a lifestyle, a passion. It's something we do because we're driven by the things we care most about.

We're driven by our love for God, and we want to share that love with others.

We're driven by our love for the Word, and we want to open that Word to hungry ears.

We're driven by our need to serve, and we serve the Church using the gifts God has given to us.

We're driven by our concern for the lost—and we're desperate to help them escape the wrath of God.

If you can sleep in on Sunday, do it. If you can come to church and sit distractedly in the pew, do that. But if you're driven by your love, your hope, your faith, and your passion to share the Hope of the world with others, then by all means, teach Sunday School.

Remember where that passion first stirred in you? Probably during a class session taught by a teacher with similar passion. Someone changed your mind with a lesson. Someone cured your hurt with a Bible promise. Someone affirmed you with an encouraging word. Someone gave life to ancient pages.

Certainly you have the freedom to accept or reject the assignment offered you. But once it turns into a heavenly commission, you have little choice. God confirms your service by the still, small voice of His Spirit or the inspired word of a Scripture passage.

You teach because of a burning zeal.

Prayer: *Lord, I obediently look and listen for your leading. May I accept your assignments with heavenly zeal. In Christ's name I pray. Amen.*

JESUS ANSWERED, "I AM THE WAY AND THE
TRUTH AND THE LIFE. NO ONE COMES TO
THE FATHER EXCEPT THROUGH ME."
—John 14:6

GOOD TEACHERS BELIEVE SOUND DOCTRINE.

DILIGENCE

*Now the Bereans were of more noble character than the Thessalonians,
for they received the message with great eagerness and examined the
Scriptures every day to see if what Paul said was true.*
—Acts 17:11

We have to do this right.

There is too much at stake for us to be haphazard in the craft of teaching Sunday School.

Lives are at stake. The eager minds that come to our classes are trying to discern the truth. It's our job to guide them in the Way.

The next generation is at stake. If knowledge of the Bible is allowed to wither, the church will suffer. Not only these students but also their children depend upon our preserving the right teaching of Scripture.

Your faith is at stake. Many teachers have succumbed to error because they were misled by false ideas. We owe it to ourselves to guard the truth. By doing so, we guard our own future.

It's acceptable for many things to be done in a merely adequate fashion. Teaching the Bible isn't one of them. We have a solemn responsibility to be skilled, to be knowledgeable, and to be thorough. Some of the greatest biblical truths will have to be dug up. Often they're buried under the casual tendencies of the age: fast food, remote control, instant-on.

The diligent student of the Word takes precious time to search the Scriptures, to grasp verses by hand that will soon be delivered by heart. Gold-mined truth can win even the coldest heart. And nuggets of convicting principles can soften the hardest heart. You must be the miner. You must not stop until you have reached the costly concepts, the hidden treasures.

We have to do this right.

Prayer: *Holy Spirit, please give me your wisdom and strength to "rightly divide" the word of truth. Be my constant companion in digging for the hidden treasures. In Jesus' name I pray. Amen.*

BEING STRENGTHENED WITH ALL POWER ACCORDING
TO HIS GLORIOUS MIGHT SO THAT YOU MAY HAVE
GREAT ENDURANCE AND PATIENCE.
—Col. 1:11

THE HOLY SPIRIT IS YOUR GUIDE.

DISCERNMENT

I am your servant; give me discernment that I may understand your statutes.
—Ps. 119:125

Inside every student is a godly man or woman trying to escape.

A great sculptor was hard at work crafting a piece of marble. A passerby asked what he was doing, and he replied, "I am releasing the angel trapped within this stone."

The artist is you. The marble quarry is your classroom. The "angels" are your students. Can you discern the godly people they *could* be if they were taught to obey the Word of God?

I know—it isn't easy. They look much different during class time. They have had too little sleep and appear drowsy. They have had too much sugar and have become hyperactive. They have had too little discipline and have become unruly. They appear to be anything but angels.

Yet they are—or they could be—if they understood the Word of God.

Teach them with patience. Teach them with diligence. Teach them with love and tenderness. Teach them with an understanding of their frailty. In other words, teach them as Jesus would. Look at them with Jesus' vision. See them standing on the shoreline waiting for the words of the Master in the boat. See those disciples crowding close to the Galilean, asking for a lesson on prayer. See that "Zacchaeus" sitting on a tree limb, afraid of the crowd but hungry for truth.

You say, "I'm not the Galilean." No, but He's your co-teacher. By His Spirit, He's in the classroom with you. Your students aren't perfect, and neither is their teacher. You're on a spiritual journey with your class. Your guide is the Holy Spirit. Your companion is the friend of the friendless.

See your students for what they really are: angels in the making.

Prayer: *Jesus, I ask you for a new vision of my class. Help me see their possibilities. In your name I pray. Amen.*

YOU, HOWEVER, KNOW ALL ABOUT MY TEACHING,
MY WAY OF LIFE, MY PURPOSE, FAITH,
PATIENCE, LOVE, ENDURANCE.
—2 Tim. 3:10

EVERY TIMOTHY NEEDS A PAUL.

MENTORING

*The things you have heard me say in the presence of many witnesses
entrust to reliable men who will also be qualified to teach others.*
—2 Tim. 2:2

Teach for life change.

Knowledge is not the goal of your teaching. It is true that we teach knowledge of the Word of God. We want our students to know each of the 66 books of the Bible, all 1,189 chapters and 31,102 verses.

Yet knowledge alone is not our goal. There's something more.

Neither is wisdom the aim of our effort. Important as wisdom is, to become shrewd or discerning is not the ultimate aim of the Bible teacher.

We teach for *life change*. We guide our students to know God. And when they come to know Him, they're changed by the power of the Holy Spirit. This is a supernatural work that goes beyond an experience of the mind or even of the heart. It's a work of God.

Teach your students well. And train them. And do one thing more: call them to be changed by the power of God. Open their eyes to the possibility of change by modeling change—by casting reflections, in word or deed, of transforming grace.

Be gentle. Often God moves as quietly as He did in the Garden of Eden. Understand that Adam and Eve didn't notice God's presence until they saw themselves naked before Him.

He must open the hearts of your students. He must show them their need of transformation. You are the mentor. Teach what you have been taught. And your changed life becomes the lesson.

Prayer: *Father, help me to teach for a change. And let me show how you have changed me. In your Son's name I pray. Amen.*

THE FRUIT OF THE SPIRIT IS LOVE, JOY, PEACE,
PATIENCE, KINDNESS, GOODNESS, FAITHFULNESS,
GENTLENESS AND SELF-CONTROL.
AGAINST SUCH THINGS THERE IS NO LAW.
—Gal. 5:22-23

YOU ARE A LIVING BIBLE TO YOUR STUDENTS.

GENTLENESS

Let your gentleness be evident to all. The Lord is near.
—Phil.4:5

*B*e kind to your students—you may be the only Bible they'll ever read.

People can be trying, and that goes double for some Sunday School students.

Questions arise for which there are no easy answers. The discussion becomes heated. Misunderstandings surface.

Students become bored and irritable.

Parents object to a teaching activity. After church, you may find yourself in a heated confrontation.

Yet these same people are God's gifts to you, a marvelous opportunity to display the love of Christ. They're people for whom the Savior died—created perfectly and redeemed completely, through faith.

What's more, you represent something they might not otherwise see: a faithful Christian. They're watching you, waiting for you to either *slip* up or *stand* up. The difference will have an everlasting impact. You'll need "outside help." You'll need the love of Christ to enfold you—and to flow through you. You'll need to be filled with the Holy Spirit. The benefit: "The fruit of the Spirit . . . love, joy, peace, patience, kindness, goodness, faithfulness, *gentleness* and self-control" (Gal. 5:22-23, emphasis added).

Perfect humans are in heaven. The rest live on the earth.

They're members of your church and sit in your Sunday School classes. They're people trying to rise above their circumstances, dealing with hidden pain, with broken relationships. They're people who have been abused. Often they act the way they do simply because that's all they've ever known.

Resist the temptation to become frustrated with the imperfect people God has placed in your care. Love them. Embrace them. Teach them. You may be their best opportunity to know Jesus.

Prayer: *Lord, thank you for giving me an opportunity to be like Jesus. In His name I pray. Amen.*

TRUST IN THE LORD WITH ALL YOUR HEART AND
LEAN NOT ON YOUR OWN UNDERSTANDING;
IN ALL YOUR WAYS ACKNOWLEDGE HIM,
AND HE WILL MAKE YOUR PATHS STRAIGHT.
—Prov. 3:5-6

FAITH CAN MOVE MOUNTAINS.

EXPECTATION

*Even though we speak like this, dear friends, we are confident of
better things in your case—things that accompany salvation.*
—Heb. 6:9

*B*elieve that you're making a difference, and you will.
There's a reason some teachers see results where others
have failed. It's because they *believe* they will.

There's a reason some teachers fail in the best of situations.
They have ability, the class has potential, but there's no fruit.
Sometimes it's because the teacher lacks vision.

If you're to succeed as a teacher of the Bible, you'll need
knowledge, skill, compassion, and spiritual power. You'll also
need faith—faith to believe that your work will be effective, to
believe that lives will be changed as a result of your efforts.

Every teacher needs the faith to believe that the lesson will
make a difference in someone's life. You'll need faith to believe
that God has equipped you to be His representative. Faith will
be needed to believe closed minds and hearts are opening up
to the teaching of God's Word.

The writer to the Hebrews says that "faith is the substance
of things hoped for" (11:1, KJV). Paul told the Christians at
Rome that "the righteous will live by faith" (Rom. 1:17). So
don't expect the journey to be constantly sunny. There will be
some shadows along the way. You must simply claim some
things by faith—including the results of your service to others.

What will be the outcome of your class this week? What will be the fruit of your labor this quarter or this year?

That all depends.

What do *you* believe it will be?

Prayer: *Father, give me eyes to see beyond the obvious—to the positive. In Jesus' name. Amen.*